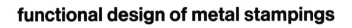

functional design of metal stampings

functional design of **metal stampings**

Federico Strasser

Published by
Society of Manufacturing Engineers
Dearborn, Michigan
1971

functional design of metal stampings

Library of Congress Catalog Card Number: 78-118843
International Standard Book Number: 0-87263-026-9

FIRST EDITION ▪ MANUFACTURING DATA SERIES

MANUFACTURED IN THE UNITED STATES OF AMERICA

preface

Metal stampings have slowly become indispensable to our high standard of living. An examination of almost any machine or gadget will reveal some metal stamping in the assembly. Today, they are used in machines, tools, all kinds of vehicles, household appliances, hardware, buildings, office equipment, retail equipment, electrical equipment, containers, clothing, and, in fact, almost every manufactured product.

During my many years of experience as an engineer in the metal stamping field and as a lecturer at various seminars, clinics, and courses conducted for the Society of Manufacturing Engineers and for the American Metal Stamping Association, I have found few single sources of information on the design of metal stampings. At one time, my previous book *Practical Design of Sheet Metal Stampings* provided the information, but it is now out of print. The present book reflects the latest thinking in the metal stamping field and tries to fill in the void in this area.

Publication of *Functional Design of Metal Stampings* would have been impossible if it were not for the help, suggestions, and data received from many friends, associates, colleagues, and pupils. Of particular help were: Johan Andersen, President of Duplicon Company, Westboro, Massachusetts, and Aldo L. Coen, Chairman of the Board of Alpha Products, Inc., Chicago, Illinois. Without their help and encouragement, the task of writing this book would have taken longer and would have been more difficult. The author is grateful to them and to the many unmentioned people for their help.

FEDERICO STRASSER

Chicago, Illinois
May, 1971

contents

CHAPTER 1 **BASIC CONCEPTS** 3
Introduction.. 3
Materials Used for Stampings 4
Checklist for Design 7
Design of Flat Stampings... 8
Design of Formed Stampings 14

CHAPTER 2 **DESIGN DETAILS** 17
How to Obtain Stampings with Low Burr Height.............. 17
Production of Holes in Stampings................................... 18
Countersinking and Counterboring................................. 20
Extruded Holes 22
Design of Shear-Formed or Lanced Tabs......................... 28
Embossed Shallow Recesses in Thin Metal Sheets.............. 34
Protrusions.. 37

CHAPTER 3 **SPECIAL CONSIDERATIONS**............................... 45
Designing for Minimum Scrap 45
Reinforcing Processes 53
Stacked Stampings... 65

CHAPTER 4 **ASSEMBLY METHODS**...................................... 73
Welded Assemblies... 73
Mechanical Assembly Methods 84

CHAPTER 5 **MISCELLANEOUS DESIGN ITEMS**..................... 99
Alignment of Stampings... 99
Relieving Screws from Bending Stresses 106
Tolerances in Metal Stampings.......................................109
Allied Operations..112
Standardization of Metal Stamping Design.......................114

CHAPTER 6 **CASE HISTORIES**...117
Practical Hints for Flat Blanks and Holes.......................117
Practical Hints for Formed Stampings.............................124
Practical Hints for Drawn Parts 129
Miscellaneous Case Histories...135
Composite Metal Stamping Designs.................................139

Conversion from Other Manufacturing Processes to
Stamping Technique..**144**
Combination Among Machining and Press Operations.........**149**

APPENDIX A..**153**

APPENDIX B..**167**
Cost Estimating of Metal Stampings..............................**167**

APPENDIX C..**173**
New, Simplified Formulas for Developed Round
Shell Blanks **173**

INDEX **177**

tables

Table I-1   Principal Field of Application for Metal Stampings........ 4

Table II-1   Necessary Punch Penetration for Severing a Low
                  Carbon Steel Slug................................. 42

Table III-1   Calculated Strength Values for Flanged Stampings........ 56

Table III-2   Rigidity Increase of Embossed Sheet Metal 62

functional design of metal stampings

basic
concepts

INTRODUCTION

In his daily life modern man employs a vast number of mass produced machines, mechanisms, tools, devices, various gadgets, and pieces of equipment which are made up totally or partially of metal stampings. For example, the average individual normally carries around on his person approximately 200 metal stampings.

According to a survey, over 100,000 metal stampings can be found in the average American home. Kitchen utensils, household machines, electrical appliances, record players, toys, tools, switches, lighting fixtures, locks, heating and air conditioning units, and bathroom articles are just a few of the more important household products made out of metal stampings (see also Table I–1).

When compared with other metalworking processes, metal stamping techniques are more successful because of the following advantages:

1) Many different kinds of metals and alloys for metal stampings are available
2) Metal stampings are light, yet strong; weight versus strength ratio is best with sheet metal
3) Part accuracy is high, resulting in interchangeability of parts
4) Low overall costs for simple manufacturing processes. This is due to ability of the process to make a complicated stamping in a few operations and to use low skilled labor. The fact that press tools have a long life, and that high stock utilization techniques are possible also help to keep overall costs low.
5) High productivity
6) The possibility of being combined with other manufacturing methods allows metal stamping techniques to take advantage of diversified production processes.

In sheet metal stamping successful products are the result of good design. Therefore, the designer is primarily responsible for improved, low-cost products. In order to keep manufacturing costs low, products should be designed with the specific requirements such as tolerances, finishes, materials, and other characteristics of the chosen manufacturing processes in mind. In other words, the design must be in accord with processing techniques.

Even if in a broad sense some three-dimensional workpieces such as forgings, cold-headed parts, and extrusions belong to metal stampings, this book is

Table I-1. Principal Field of Application for Metal Stampings.

Machines and Tools	Machine elements, machine tool components, tools, tool components, sewing machines, automatic machines, agricultural implements, material handling equipment, lawn mowers, fans, typewriters, office machines, control instruments, pulleys, turbine blades, textile machinery
Household Appliances	Furniture, washing machines, burners, stoves, ranges, furnaces, radiators, heaters, refrigerators, kitchenware, cooking utensils, saucepans, kettles, egg poachers, can openers, cutlery, tea pots, waffle irons, toasters, vacuum cleaners, wash tubs, bath tubs, sinks, radio, TV sets, record players, tape recorders, hair dryers, lamps, lanterns, bells, gongs, baby carriages, mail boxes, cigarette boxes and cases, trays, ash trays, safety razor blades, electric razors
Clothing	Buttons, eyelets, buckles
Vehicles	Airplanes, automobiles, motor cars, bicycles, railway coaches, tanks, tractors, wheels for vehicles
Hardware	Building hardware, door knobs, locks, pipe couplings, hinges, bathroom and kitchen fixtures, light metal sash, garbage cans
Buildings	Houses, roofing, bridges, cement reinforcements
Office	Adding machines, advertising novelties, calendars, tags, envelope clasps
Shops	Cash registers, cash boxes, menu holders, toys, jewelry, cameras
Electricity	Motors, generators, transformers, wiring devices (switches, receptacles, lampholders), meters and measuring instruments, telephone, telegraph, electronics, electrical conduit, stripping devices, lighting fixtures
Containers	Cans, tin boxes, drums, drum lids, caps, buckets, canisters; containers for food, for medicinal purposes, and for chemical materials
Miscellaneous	Guns, cartridges, coins, medals, insignia, bird cages, caskets, coffins, watches, collapsible tubes, dental instruments, metal signs, musical instruments, shovels, thimbles, art metal trades, capsules

limited to the study of components made from two-dimensional metal sheets, i.e., where the third dimension — thickness — is negligible in comparison to width and length.

MATERIALS USED FOR STAMPINGS

The steel industry is the prime supplier of the metal used for metal stampings. About 56 percent of all steel produced by the industry is sold in the form of sheets. This sheet metal is primarily the raw material used in metal stampings. The following is a list of the characteristics and requirements necessary in raw materials to be used for stampings or press work:

1) Comparatively low cost
2) High strength. Rolled sheets are generally stronger than cast metals; consequently, the higher specific strength permits thinner walls and less weight.
3) Good surface finish. Materials are often used "as rolled" because of their smooth, satisfactory surfaces.
4) Uniformity of crystalline metal structure
5) Uniformity of dimensions
6) Easy workability.

The variety of raw materials that can be used for metal stampings is much greater than for machined or otherwise produced parts. In the majority of cases, the strength of the material is only one reason for the choice; other features such as easy formability, pleasing appearance, and safe performance often play an important part when making the choice. Essentially, every material that can be produced in the shape of sheets or strips and that will not shatter under impact can be worked with press-tools (at least in the simpler operations). Excluded are only the very brittle materials such as cast iron, glass, and similar materials.

Materials used in stamping generally fall into one of three groups: ferrous metals, nonferrous metals, and nonmetallic materials.

Ferrous Metals

All those alloys whose chief element is iron belong in this group. If no other special requirements exist, the first choice of material to be used for stamping should be low carbon (.05 to .20 percent C) cold-rolled or hot-rolled steel. Cold-rolled steel (CRS) comes in gages up to $\frac{1}{16}$ in., while hot-rolled steel (HRS) is available in heavier gages. More low carbon steels are used for stampings than all other materials combined. No better nor more economical material is available.

Sometimes certain specifications or considerations must be met in order to increase the material strength and resistance to particularly adverse conditions (oxidation, corrosion, heat, etc.). Therefore, alloy steels such as high carbon steels, silicon steels, stainless steels, and heat-resistant steels are often used in stampings. These alloys, however, are often more difficult to work in presses, especially during forming operations. For this reason, their shape tolerances must be rather wide.

Nonferrous Metals

Aluminum in a wide range of alloys and tempers is used quite often for stampings. Copper and its alloys of brass, beryllium copper, phosphor bronze, cupronickel, and nickel silver are also often used. Magnesium and its alloys, zinc and its alloys, titanium and its alloys, nickel and its alloys are also widely used. Other nonferrous metals include the "wonder" or "space age" metals of zirconium, tantalum, niobium, tungsten, molybdenum, vanadium along with their alloys; and the precious metals of gold, silver, platinum, and palladium, along with their alloys.

Prefinished Metal Sheets

Metal sheets, especially low-carbon steel and aluminum, can be obtained with some protective or decorative coatings. Cold-rolled steel that has been zinc coated by a hot dip process is called galvanized steel. If the steel is tin coated, it is often referred to as tin-plate. When the galvanized sheets are heat-treated after the coating process, the steel is galvannealed and becomes a zinc-iron alloy.

Zinc coated CRS sheets treated by an electrolytic process are called electro-galvanized steel sheets. Phosphatized galvanized sheets have been chemically processed with a primer coat for a subsequent painting operation. Terne sheets are CRS sheets that have been coated with an alloy of 85 percent lead and 15 percent tin.

Aluminum coated CRS sheets are coated by immersion in molten aluminum. A No. 1 sheet is heat resistant, while a No. 2 sheet is corrosion resistant. Clad metal consists of a sheet metal base intimately covered through a mechanical process by a layer of another kind of metal or alloy. Many clad combinations are available. The most usual ones are: steel plus stainless steel, nickel, or copper; silver-copper plus stainless steel or some precious metal; brass plus some precious metal; and aluminum plus an aluminum alloy.

Prepainted sheets come in many colors. Sheets preplated by chromium, nickel, copper, brass, cadmium, and precious metals are also available. Some metal sheets are printed by lithography; others are plastic coated, and some are coated with thin paper for protection of a highly finished or polished surface. Additionally, some metal sheets are used with other than smooth surfaces. The most usual forms are perforated metals, expanded metals, and embossed metals.

Nonmetallic Materials

The possibilities and economic conveniences of using press-tools for the production of parts made from nonmetallic materials are too often overlooked. Dies of standard design can be used for those nonmetallic materials of a sufficient consistency and hardness, while so-called dinking or hollow dies (similar to cookie cutters) are used for softer materials.

Nonmetallic materials may be classified into two groups: natural and artificial. To the first group belong: paper, cardboard, leather, rawhide, hard rubber, soft rubber, cork, mica, asbestos, felt, fabric, and wood. To the second group belong: plastics, celluloid, vulcanized sheet fiber, Masonite,* linoleum, etc.

Thicknesses

The thickness of sheet metal employed for metal and nonmetallic stampings varies widely from foils as thin as .003 in. up to $\frac{1}{2}$ in. or even more. However, the majority of stampings are made from thicknesses ranging between .020 and .080 in.

Unfortunately there are no standards for defining the expressions "light," "medium," and "heavy" when defining the gage of metal sheets. According to an arbitrary classification, sheets up to .031 in. are considered as light gage, sheets from .031 to .109 in. as medium gage, and over .109 in. as heavy gage.

---

*Reg TM, Masonite Corporation.

Metals for Drawing and Severe Forming

These metals deserve special mention because of the highly exacting properties which are demanded for both drawing and for severe forming operations.

Only a few metals can be successfully subjected to a drawing operation. For drawing, the metal must possess great ductility combined with comparatively high tensile strength. In other words, the metal must have a high elongation and an ample spread between yield point where the metal takes a permanent set and the ultimate strength where it breaks. Among the ordinary metals having these properties and therefore are being employed for drawn components are steel, brass, copper, aluminum, and zinc.

The best stamping steel usually has the following specifications:

1) Quality: CRS 1008 FAK DQ
2) Chemical analysis: .05 to .08C; .25 to .50Mn; .05 maximum P; .05 maximum S
3) Hardness: R_b 40 to 44
4) Ductility (Olsen): .400 to .500
5) Tensile strength: 35,000 to 45,000 psi
6) Elongation: 38 to 46 percent.

Precious metals have better drawing characteristics than ordinary metals but cannot be utilized on a large scale for industrial or domestic uses.

CHECKLIST FOR DESIGN

Before estimating the cost of producing a given stamping, all blueprints and specifications concerning that stamping must be checked, and if necessary, carefully revised. The checking method employed by any given company depends on its individual characteristics, set-up, and tradition. The following basic procedures have been found practical, efficient, and satisfactory:

1) Check the blueprint strictly as a drawing, i.e., from the draftsman's standpoint
2) Check the blueprint, specifications, and instructions from the designer's standpoint
3) And if necessary, suggest changes accordingly.

Blueprints

First, ascertain whether the drawing is complete or not. Some posting of dimensions and specifications may have been overlooked. In addition, all dimensions on drawings should always be posted so that no calculations will be necessary in the shop.

Other mistakes can be made too. For instance, sometimes an incorrect view or projection on the drawing may cause problems if not caught in time. On up or down scaled drawings, the actual dimensional values and not the correctly scaled dimensions can mistakenly be posted.

All abbreviations on the drawing should have perfectly clear meanings. In case of even the slightest doubt, correct meanings should be established or spelled out in full. Steel specifications are usually a series of initials with conventional meanings. Here is a typical case:

16 GA HRPO, CQ AK, SAE 1010 SHEET

Where: 16 GA   = .0598 in. mean thickness
         HRPO   = hot rolled pickled and oiled
         CQ   = commercial quality
         AK   = aluminum killed
         SAE 1010 = plain low-carbon steel with about .10 percent carbon
                    content

Finally, the checker must be sure that the blueprint has the latest revision and that the revisions are all properly recorded.

Design

After being satisfied that the blueprints and specifications are correct and complete, the design itself must correspond to sound, correct principles and techniques. Many points have to be checked. The following list of design parameters contains only the chief details to consider:

1) Quantities needed – this influences expected useful life of tooling and other design concepts
2) Stock – quality, temper, low cost, low scrap – use standard gage sheet; strip-steel or sheets of nonstandard thicknesses should be employed only if absolutely necessary
3) Size – sometimes there are limitations of size, space, weight, etc.
4) Strength – part must resist loads and stresses in function and in handling
5) Critical dimensions – specify tolerances separately for each dimension of the part (loose or close according to functional and/or assembly requirements)
6) Take into account needs for flatness, squareness, parallelism, and concentricity
7) Sharp corners in cutting contours must be avoided
8) Burr height specified if functionally important
9) Finishes and esthetics
10) Allied operations
11) Inspection
12) Assembly method.

DESIGN OF FLAT STAMPINGS

Stamped Links

In many cases the holes in a metal stamping are the most interesting and most important features. Their quantity, size, location, tolerances, surface finish, and other characteristics are the determining factors in the workpiece design. The surrounding metal connects the holes, locates them, and of course, gives the strength necessary to the part. This means that in these cases the outer shape or contour of the part has no importance at all; the designer has ample liberty of action in this respect. Links are typical of the above description and are used when two identical holes must be located at a given distance.

When estimating tooling costs, stamped links are an important consideration. The designer of mechanical parts is not supposed to design the press-tools which will be used for the production of the stampings he designs; however, he should be able to visualize the dies needed for every production method so he can estimate the cost of producing his stampings. In its turn, the method of producing a part is governed to a great extent by its design as well as by the other characteristics such as tolerances, quantities, etc.

The straight, square piece illustrated in Fig. 1–1 is the least expensive shape to design and produce. It takes less material to produce straight ends, and they

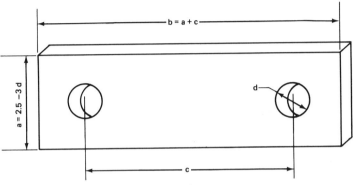

Fig. 1–1.

require simpler, less expensive dies. Additionally, straight end designs have cost advantages for the following reasons: slight inaccuracies in the location of the punched holes in the components are practically unavoidable due to the commercial width tolerances of the bar stock and the tolerances required by shearing the strips from the sheets. Such an eccentric position of the holes remains unperceived in the case of straight ends; in the case of half-round or other types of ends, it is quite noticeable.

A very simple esthetic improvement of the link shape consists of chamfering the corners (see Fig. 1–2). This shape requires some additional notching operations incorporated into the corresponding dies.

Fig. 1–2.

With a somewhat more elaborate and more expensive tool, the corners are rounded instead of chamfered. In these cases, never try to blend the rounding with the sides. Such a design as illustrated in Fig. 1–3 is wrong. It requires expensive tooling, costly operation, and very close tolerances in the stock width. The corner radii should always be larger than the distance from the ends (Fig. 1–4 is right), or a proper clearance of 10 to 15 deg should be provided as indicated in Fig. 1–5.

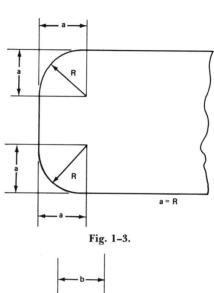

a = R

Fig. 1–3.

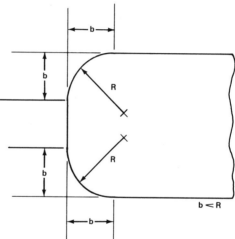

b < R

Fig. 1–4.

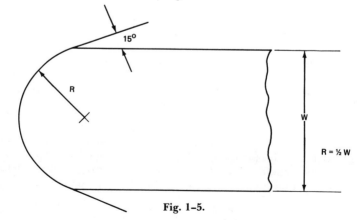

15°

R = ½ W

Fig. 1–5.

In some cases it is not practical to use the above described production methods. The chief conditions which may require that the strips have the transversal cross-sectional area of the links (thickness × width, instead of thickness × length) are these:

1) Parts are too long. The strips become too heavy and cumbersome to handle, especially with heavy gage stock.
2) The longitudinal edges must be rounded or otherwise mill finished
3) One or both ends must be specially shaped
4) The same tool (universal type tooling) must be used for different, but similar parts.

A "parting" tool (see Fig. 1–6) is the simplest type of tool. At each press-stroke, this tool shapes one end of each of two subsequent parts and simultaneously punches the holes in each end so that at each press-stroke one complete part is produced.

Referring to the end shape of the links produced with tools of the kind shown in Fig. 1–6, the designer should keep in consideration the same principles as explained above. First preference should be given to straight ends, unless for some important functional reason this is not possible. Then use chamfered ends or rounded corners.

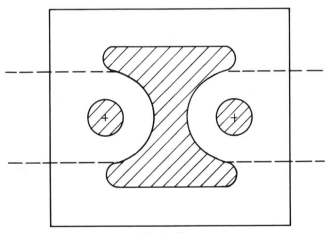

Fig. 1–6.

Many designers prefer fully rounded link ends, for example, when the parts are mounted side by side, such as in electrical bus-bars, and small length inaccuracies are not so evident. This design is not practical, because it requires a die which is more expensive to build. The parts are unnecessarily weaker and besides, the smallest unavoidable inaccuracy or irregularity in the parting operation, has an unfavorable consequence on the esthetic appearance of the workpieces. Therefore, this design should be avoided. If for some special, important reasons the ends must be rounded, then take into account the following basic rule:

Do not blend the rounding with the side contour lines (Fig. 1–7 is not economical). As in case of Fig. 1–3 this means unnecessarily high tooling and operational costs. Easy solutions are shown in Figs. 1–5 and 1–8. In Fig. 1–8, the

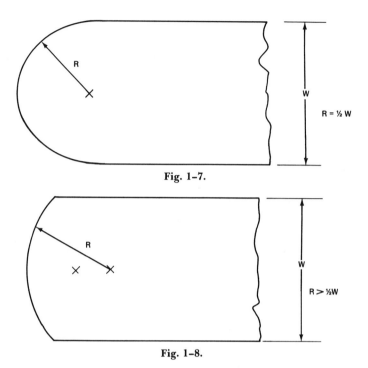

Fig. 1-7.

Fig. 1-8.

rounding radius is larger than half of the part's width. In Fig. 1-5, the radius is equal to half of the part's width, but the end shape is an incomplete semicircle with an inclination of about 10 to 15 deg on each side.

The production methods described up to this point are employed for parts with ample dimensional tolerances in the blank contour and size. This is the usual case. However, sometimes in addition to other specifications such as hole size and center distances, the part length must also be held within certain tolerance limits. In such cases the so-called "strip-blanking" method is used. This consists of working with strips of the right dimensions and employing a tool which cuts the two ends of a given part *simultaneously*. Fig. 1-9 illustrates this principle showing a progressive tool for transversal strips and chamfered ends.

Another case, analogous to link design is portrayed in Figs. 1-10 and 1-11. Three holes of a given size had to be located in a stamping of a given pattern. The first, elementary solution consists of taking a rectangular piece of sheet metal and punching holes in it in the right quantity, size, shape, and location (see Fig.

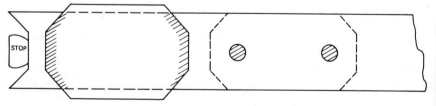

Fig. 1-9.

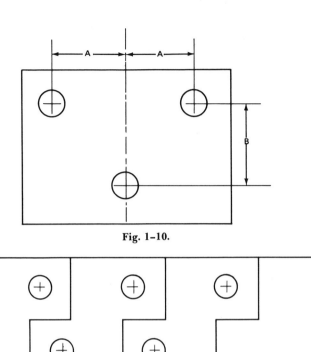

Fig. 1-10.

Fig. 1-11.

1-10). This is the way to make a few dozens or hundreds of pieces. For mass production, the stamping's outer contour may be changed in shape. In this case, the outer shape is immaterial making for a very economical "scrapless" strip-layout (see Fig. 1-11) that realizes a substantial stock savings of 40 percent.

Shaped Flat Stampings

Unfortunately, only in the minority of cases is the outer shape of stampings totally immaterial. In the majority of cases, the outer contour becomes partly or totally functional, and thus it must comply with certain requirements or specifications.

Such requirements may be either negative or positive. The first one means clearance for moving or stationary components; the second one means matching, intermeshing, or in some way contacting portions of other components.

If the general configuration, accuracy, and other characteristics permit, preference should be given to cutting off or parting design, because of the several economical and technical advantages offered by such a design (Fig. 1-12).

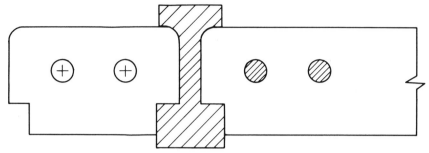

Fig. 1-12.

Blanked Flat Stampings

When the design involves a more complicated, outer contour, closer dimensional tolerances, heavier gage stock, and other higher performance requirements, it is necessary to fully blank out the stamping from sheet, strip, or coil material.

In the design of the outer shape of fully blanked stampings, the designer must consider all the basic rules and recommendations demanded by sound, practical, and economic production techniques. The main points to keep in mind in this respect are: simple shapes; preference for straight contour lines; avoidance of sharp corners and details which require weak and/or delicate tool members.

DESIGN OF FORMED STAMPING

Bent Parts

In the evolution of metal stamping technique, the next step consists in transforming a two-dimensional piece in which the thickness of sheet metal is negligible in comparison to width and length into a three-dimensional object. This may be done by several methods. The easiest and most common way is to bend up one or more sides of the flat blank.

Bent or formed details on a component may be necessary in a stamping for reinforcement, for safety to eliminate injury from sharp edges, for ease of assembly, or for esthetics.

In the design of formed parts several basic and special details must be taken into consideration. The chief ones are: sheet lamination direction, burr side, rounding radii, flat blank contour, springback phenomenon, leg height, and nesting of stampings. Nesting will be discussed in Chapter 6.

Formed Boxes

When all the sides of a rectangular or polygonal part are bent up, a box is formed. For light duty, the junction gaps are left open. For heavy duty and/or in those cases when the box must be tight, the corners are welded, brazed, or soldered.

Drawn Shells and Boxes

Seamless hollow vessels may be formed directly from sheet metal by the process of drawing. Both the cross-sectional and the longitudinal section may be chosen from several shapes. Among possible combinations the cylindrical, flangeless cup is the most common and most frequent (and the easiest to produce). When designing drawn shells, especially geometrically regular shapes, the designer must strive for a combination of low height, large diameter, and heavy gage stock, the most favorable conditions for achieving the easiest operation.

Stacked Stampings

The last step in the evolution of metal stamping techniques is the production of simulated solid three-dimensional objects by means of the so-called stacking method.

A stacked stamping consists essentially of a rigid assembly of several individual sheet metal stampings, sometimes with the addition of some machined or otherwise produced parts. The laminations may be identical or different in shape and/or size. By intelligent combination of these elements, many workpieces which normally are produced by machining, casting, forging, or other methods may be made with sheet metal stampings. Thus, the low cost of press-working the metals is substituted for more costly manufacturing methods (for more details see Chapter 4).

Stacked stamping is not new. For many years it has been employed in electrical machines, transformers, padlocks, and other fields. Lately, however, designers have widely adopted stacked stamping techniques.

design details

HOW TO OBTAIN STAMPINGS WITH LOW BURR HEIGHT

A burr is an unwanted, sharp, uneven ridge or protruding roughness around the periphery of a hole or the outer contour of a blank caused by the displacement of metal as the result of a cutting operation.

Every cutting action performed by a die progressively dulls the die cutting edges. Consequently, after a certain number of operations, the burr height around the outer contour of blanks and the periphery of punched holes begins to become more pronounced. This is a natural process with no exceptions to the following rule: production of a stamping absolutely free of burrs is impossible.

While the burr height remains below certain limits, it does no harm, but when it becomes excessive, the cutting edges of the die must be sharpened. There is no consensus as to the allowable burr height limit, which varies with each case, each company, and each stamping. It depends on such varied factors as: the function and use of the part, the appearance of the burr, the magnitude and number of subsequent operations, danger of cuts to operators and users, considerations of surface finish such as scratches on the stamping surface, considerations of tool care such as scratches on the tool members, and whether or not the part can be stacked for storage.

The quantity of hits performed by a cutting press tool between resharpenings is determined chiefly by the maximum burr height permitted on the stamping. Burr height is usually the same at the hole periphery or outer blank contour, as it is on the corresponding slug; hence, the burr is usually measured on the slug itself.

Burrs are especially undesirable for laminations on electrical motors and transformers, both because of the danger of magnetic shorts and because they reduce the space utilization factor by using additional space when stacked.

As mentioned before, industry has no standards for allowable burr height. The usual practice is to accept a burr up to:
1) 10 percent of material thickness in the case of light gage stock
2) 5 percent of material thickness in case of heavy gage stock
3) In no case more than .006 in. although many companies have a limit of .005 in.
4) .001 in. is always acceptable, even if it is more than 10 percent of stock thickness when stock is less than .010 in. thick.

In the majority of cases, burrs of such heights may be left on the stampings

17

since usually they are not bothersome. If they cannot be left on the stampings, burr removal is easily performed automatically, quickly and inexpensively by tumbling or vibratory finishing.

Removal of burrs higher than these specified limits means a more expensive operation, especially in certain cases. Burr height *alone* is no definitive criterion for ease of removal (possibility of removal by tumbling). It is much easier to remove a high and thin burr than a low but wide one. Consequently, the best policy is to control the formation of burrs so that they can be held under reasonable, acceptable values. Burr formation is controlled through good stamping design and tool maintenance.

The stamping design has a decided influence on burr formation. Sharp corners, sharp points, narrow slots, etc. are stress-concentration points; they cause a more rapid wear of the tool cutting edges than simple, regular cutting shapes, and so they accelerate the formation of burrs. Consequently, the component designer should always try to avoid unsatisfactory contour details.

An arbitrary classification of cutting shapes, starting from those which cause the least tool wear to those which cause greater tool wear, is as follows: circles, ellipses, oblongs, keyholes, rectangles with rounded corners, rectangles with sharp corners, narrow slots, rhomboids, and acute angle contour details with sharp corners.

Sometimes dimensional tolerances will also have an influence on burr formation. If a hole must be punched at a very accurate, small distance from other holes within the stamping contour, the holes must be punched simultaneously with one tool. If the distance between holes is too small, the tool life is shortened considerably, and thus, burr formation will tend to increase rapidly.

Characteristics of the material used also have a direct influence on the burr formation rate. In a broad sense, higher strength metals have less tendency for burr formation. Softer metals do not lend themselves to cutting operations as readily as harder stock. Consequently, the softer metals have a greater tendency to form burrs.

High ductility is, within certain limits, a disadvantage from the burr formation standpoint. Material of drawing quality has higher tendency to form burrs than steel sheet of commercial quality. Anyway, homogeneity of structure improves cutting conditions, and therefore, lessens the tendency to form burrs.

Finally, thin stock, especially in case of comparatively large stampings, has a greater tendency of bowing, and therefore, a higher burr formation rate. This tendency may be compensated by blankholding devices, shedders, pads, etc.

PRODUCTION OF HOLES IN STAMPINGS

The majority of holes in metal stampings are round. These holes may be either punched with press tools or drilled and reamed. If necessary, nonround holes are practically always punched. Sometimes a combination of these operations is needed. The most appropriate production method depends on the characteristics of the hole, especially its size in relation to stock thickness and quality, and the shape and finish of the hole walls.

Punching a hole in a flat stamping (Fig. 2–1) is the less expensive method. However, this is possible only if the diameter of the hole is not too small in rela-

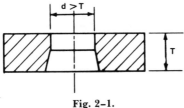

Fig. 2-1.

tion to stock thickness. No hard or fast rules exist regarding the minimal limit of holes that can be safely and consistently punched in mass production stamping; they depend chiefly on the following characteristics:

1) Properties of stock
2) Design of punch: (a) especially stiff support of the cutting point close to the die plate, i.e., the top surface of the stock; (b) short cutting point, and (c) some special forms of the cutting point to relieve cutting force
3) Design of stripper
4) Punch clearance up to double or more of standard values
5) Ample die clearance
6) Craftsmanship in tool building: (a) spotless finish of punch and die; (b) perfect alignment through the even distribution of punch clearance, and (c) perfect stripping conditions (perpendicularity)
7) Tool steel for the punch. It should have high compressive strength and be high impact or shock resistant
8) Type of press. A shock-free hydraulic press is better than a mechanical punch press.

As a rule of thumb, the minimal diameter for round punches as well as for nonround punches is:

1) For low strength stock such as aluminum with a shearing strength of up to 25,000 psi and a tensile strength of up to 32,000 psi—equal to stock thickness
2) For medium strength stock such as brass and 1010 steel with a shearing strength of 25,000 to 75,000 psi and a tensile strength of 32,000 to 95,000 psi—$1\frac{1}{2}$ times stock thickness
3) For high strength stock such as stainless steel and high carbon steel with a shearing strength of over 75,000 psi and a tensile strength of over 95,000 psi—twice stock thickness
4) In no case less than .062 in.—smaller sizes are technically feasible but entail additional costs and difficulties in production.

A punched hole (see Fig. 2-2) maintains the nominal diameter of the punch for only 20 to 35 percent of the thickness of the metal, depending also on the punch clearance, and the shear strength of the metal. A heavier stock will produce a proportionately shorter land, while a softer stock will produce a longer land. If a finished hole is desired through the entire stock thickness, the hole is punched undersize and then either shaved to size with another die or redrilled and reamed (see Fig. 2-3).

When the hole is too small for punching (d/t ratio is under the limits specified above), a usually more expensive method must be used (see Fig. 2-4). In this case, the hole must be drilled, deburred, and sometimes also reamed.

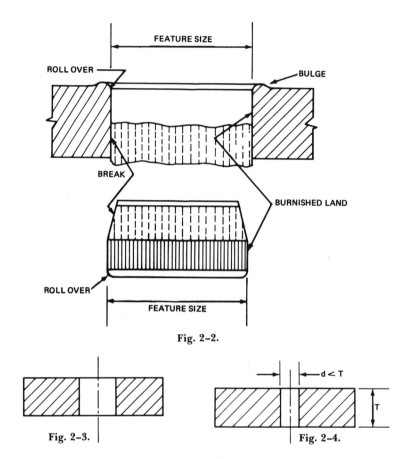

Fig. 2-2.

Fig. 2-3.

Fig. 2-4.

COUNTERSINKING AND COUNTERBORING

If the heads of the screws or rivets are not permitted to protrude above the stamping surface, special steps must be taken. If the fastener head is a flat one (tapered toward the shaft), the surface is countersunk. If the head bottom forms a right angle with the shaft, the surface is counterbored.

In case of light gage stock up to .062 in., the conical cavity whether beveled or flared is formed with press tools. Under favorable conditions and with properly designed dies, the clearance hole is punched simultaneously when forming the depression (see Fig. 2-5).

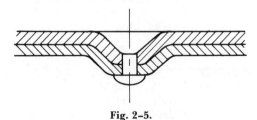

Fig. 2-5.

Chamfering or shallow swaged countersinking can be performed with press tools if the depth of chamfer does not exceed 10 to 20 percent of stock thickness in case of light stock, and 20 to 30 percent in case of heavy gage material (see Fig. 2–6). This is a comparatively inexpensive method. Deeper swaged chamfers mean a more difficult and more expensive operation.

In case of heavy stock over .125 in. thick, the deep, tapered recess for the fastener head is made with proper cutting tools such as milling cutters. It is necessary to avoid feather edges at the hole bottom by leaving a short parallel portion (see Fig. 2–7).

In case of light gage stock, counterbored cavities are press formed. Also in such cases, it is possible to combine in one common tool the punching of the clearance holes with the forming of the depression (see Fig. 2–8).

Analogous to Fig. 2–7, in the case of heavy stock the counterbored cavity is produced in machine tools with proper cylindrical milling cutters or boring tools as shown in Fig. 2–9.

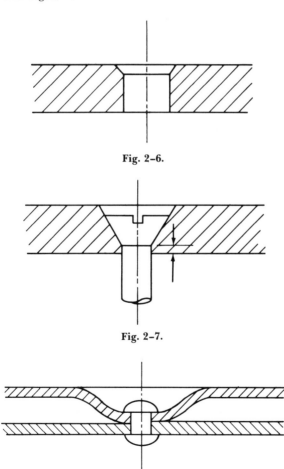

Fig. 2–6.

Fig. 2–7.

Fig. 2–8.

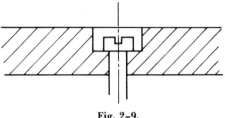

Fig. 2-9.

Countersinking, counterboring, and deep chamfering are expensive operations. The designer should make use of them only if and when they are unavoidable.

EXTRUDED HOLES

An inexpensive, simple way of increasing the length of a hole in a sheet metal stamping is to form an integral, extended collar around the hole. This is then called an extruded, collared, flanged, embossed, or drifted hole.

Extruded holes are widely used in a variety of ways, most frequently in light machinery, instruments, home appliances, toys, radiators, vehicles, and electric wiring devices. The bosses may be formed in practically any kind and shape of metal stamping; they may be formed not only on flat surfaces, but also on curved, bent, or drawn surfaces.

Assembly

In the majority of cases, extruded holes are used for joining two components, one of which is a sheet metal stamping with the extruded hole. Metal stamped components are joined together in the following ways:

1) Tapping the extruded and embossed hole, and using the hole as a nut is the simplest and most common way of assembling two components to each other. Thus, the bearing length of the nut becomes twice or more as much as the sheet metal thickness, and consequently, the strength of the joint is increased considerably (see Fig. 2-10).

2) The boss may be utilized as a hollow rivet for joining two thin sheet

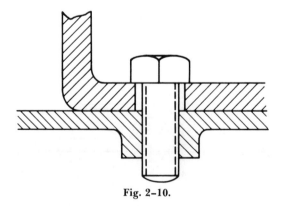

Fig. 2-10.

metal components. The free end of the boss is simply flared or swaged out, creating a firm joint. Common eyelets belong basically to this application (see Fig. 2–11).

3) If the dimensions of the boss with respect to stock thickness of the counterpart stamping are favorable, then the joining may be made by curling the boss end

4) A piece of tubing may be joined with an embossed hole by means of a proper bead which acts as a stop and flaring out or half-curling the free end of the pipe

5) A solid shaft is assembled with an extruded hole by crimping the boss into a proper groove machined in the shaft; small flanges for coupling two shafts are sometimes made in this way (see Fig. 2–12)

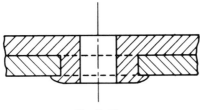

Fig. 2–11.

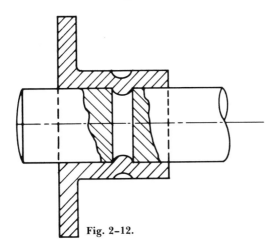

Fig. 2–12.

6) Proper guide for full riveting of reduced shafts are provided by extruded holes (see Fig. 2–13)

7) For limited strength conditions, simple press-fit or interference fit may be used for joining a full shaft or a piece of pipe with a sheet metal stamping provided with a flanged hole. For increasing the strength and torsional resistance, a straight knurling of the shaft end is recommended

8) Soldering, brazing, and welding are extensively used for joining tubings or solid shafts with embossed holes. Fig. 2–14 shows one of a great variety of possible designs

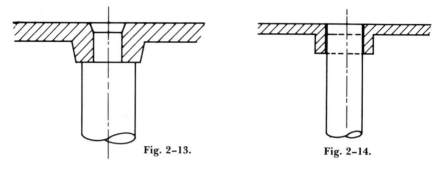

Fig. 2–13.   Fig. 2–14.

9) Sometimes, when disassembly of the joint is required and the overall
dimensions are favorable, the flange may be fastened to the shaft with a
cylindrical or tapered dowel pin

10) Spool ends are often made from sheet metal in the form of extruded
flanges, and they are joined with the bosses of the cylinder by crimping,
lapping, etc. (see Fig. 2–15)

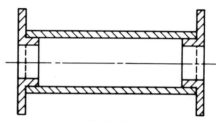

Fig. 2–15.

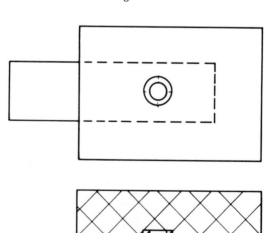

Fig. 2–16.

11) Thin metal inserts may be anchored in plastic moldings, die castings, or concrete by embossing a hole in the metal insert, and embedding the hole in the plastic molding etc. (see Fig. 2–16).

Bearings

Small revolving shafts must have a certain amount of contacting surface in their bearings, according to loads, speeds, and working conditions of the shaft. In many watches, instruments, and light machinery, lengthening the bearing area by doubling the boss to twice stock thickness and smoothing the entire hole surface will often provide the required bearing surface. In some light duty cases, the outer surface of the boss replaces the pivoting shaft (see Fig. 2–17).

Alignment

The boss may be used for locating aligning dowel pins in one or both of the sheet metal components. In some instances, the outer surface of the boss may substitute for the dowel pin. Then the boss enters matching punched or embossed holes in the counterpart for aligning the two components (see Fig. 2–18).

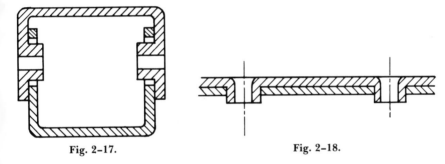

Fig. 2–17.   Fig. 2–18.

Reinforcing

Plates and sheets may be notably reinforced, and their stability and rigidity considerably increased by judicious and reasonable use of strategically located holes in the panels.

Protection

There are several applications of extruded holes for prevention of accidents and damage to equipment.
1) Grommets are rolled holes in sheet metals, formed round so that electrical wires, cables, and other kinds of cords may be drawn through them without damaging the outer insulations; such applications may be found in radio sets, electrical outlets, and other electrical appliances (see Fig. 2–19). The first step for grommet forming is the creation of extruded holes
2) Extruded holes are also used for creating rough, anti-slipping surfaces such as industrial floor sections and jeep floorboards

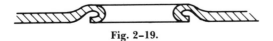

Fig. 2–19.

3) Cylinders of laundry and drycleaning machines are made from extruded sheet for the free passage of liquids. The inner surfaces must be smooth and rounded to prevent buttons and hooks from being caught by the hole edges.

Miscellaneous

1) Graters—there are many domestic and industrial devices and machines that need a rough surface for grating such as potato peeling machines, and surface roughening equipment

2) Gages—by properly joining with a press-fit, brazing, or welding and further machining of two matching extruded flanges, an excellent female gage is made. In actual practice, such gages have given very satisfactory performance (see Fig. 2–20)

3) Decoration—sometimes sheets with extruded holes are used for ornamental purposes. In these cases, however, the pattern is usually made with other than round holes.

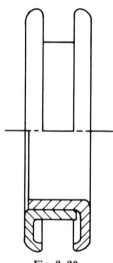

Fig. 2–20.

Other than Round Bosses

Most extruded holes are round. In those cases where the bosses are not round, they are formed in the same way as cylindrical holes are formed. However, it is necessary to determine by means of practical trials the shape and dimensions of the corresponding tool members.

Calculations

Determination of the dimensions of various details such as maximum boss height, diameter of the preliminary hole, and the radius of the die opening are based upon simple theoretical considerations, corroborated by findings of practical experience and systematic research.

The start of the calculations is the assumption that the ring $T(d_2 - d)$ is transformed into a cylindrical sharp-edged boss (see Fig. 2–21). This means that the corresponding volumes should be equal as stated in Eq. 2–1:

$$\frac{\pi T(d_2^2 - d^2)}{4} = \frac{\pi H_t(d_2^2 - d_1^2)}{4} \tag{2-1}$$

The theoretical height of the extruded hole is stated in Eq. 2–2:

$$H_t = T\frac{d_2^2 - d^2}{d_2^2 - d_1^2} \tag{2-2}$$

Under normal conditions the actual cross-sectional shape of an extruded hole is never cylindrical, straight, or square as shown at the left side of Fig. 2–21. There are two chief reasons for the difference between theory and practice. First, due to the considerable stretching of material, the outer side of the boss tends to become tapered, and toward its end its thickness is much smaller than the original stock gage. In addition, there is also an unavoidable rounding at the top (see right side of Fig. 2–21). Consequently, the boss is practically always longer than what Eq. 2-2 indicates. The length increase depends chiefly on the

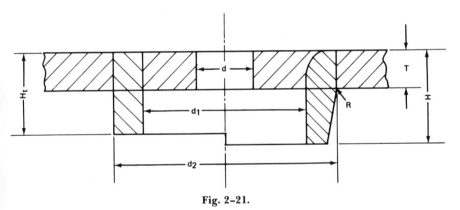

Fig. 2–21.

quality of material and the ratio of flange diameter to material thickness. Only practical trials can determine exactly what the actual height should be.

An important point to consider is that the length of extruded holes is not simply two or three times the material thickness as it would appear from Fig. 2–21 (ratio H/T). Actually, it is much more. In fact, the internal walls of extruded holes are almost entirely smooth, parallel, and concentric except for the small rounding at the top. In an ordinary punched hole only a small fraction of the material thickness is smooth, parallel, and concentric (the land, see Fig. 2–2). Thus, if the hole is used as a bearing, the actual working surface of extruded holes becomes a heavy multiple of a corresponding standard punched hole (the higher the material thickness, the better becomes the ratio).

The diameter of the preliminary (pilot) hole d depends primarily on the stock quality and stock thickness:

$$d = d_1 \div 1.20 \text{ to } 1.30 \tag{2-3}$$

Practice teaches that the radius of the die ring edge rounding (see Fig. 2–21) may be as small as .05 d_3 up to as large as .5 d_3. The correct selection depends on design requirements and performance.

To prevent any critical distortions, leave enough flat material around an extruded hole. For best results, the minimum distance from the stamping edge to outer boss edge should be four times material thickness. The outer boss edge distance between two neighboring holes should be at least six times material thickness and in no case less than $1/16$ in.

DESIGN OF SHEAR-FORMED OR LANCED TABS

In the design of stampings for light products made from sheet metal components, a very versatile construction element known as internal tabs may be employed. They are also known as ears, flaps, lugs, prongs, legs, or projections and are formed in the sheet metal parts. Several economic advantages such as reduced material employment, decreased labor costs, reduced weight, and reduced tooling costs can be realized through the use of these tabs. The application of shear-formed or lanced tabs is extensive and varied as the examples below will indicate.

Fastening

The most widely used application for lanced tabs is fastening, i.e., for permanent (rarely for semi-permanent or even temporary) assembly of components. Other methods utilize lanced lugs for fastening purposes. One method of fastening is called folding or lapping, which is discussed in detail in Chapter 4.

Another method is bending or curving around a round (or polygonal) shaft (armored cable, etc.); this lanced tab will locate and hold the shaft quite firmly (see Fig. 2–22). An analogous design is the forming of lanced bridges where both ends of the tab remain attached to the parent metal sheet (see Fig. 2–23). Occasionally, alternate bridge designs are tapped. Several commercial fasteners use some lanced tab detail that contributes substantially to the efficiency of the fastening function. From the numberless possible and actual designs, two of the most characteristic fasteners are: the well-known flat type speed nut which is formed by lancing and shaping the two opposite arched prongs in the sheet metal, and speed clips, used in combination with smooth, unthreaded studs, rivets, tubings, or nails, which are made in the same way. The only difference is in the shape of the tabs.

Shear-formed tabs are often used to fasten a panel or other component to a wall. Fig. 2–24 illustrates a typical bracket of this kind.

If the stock is sufficiently thick, then the flap may be riveted or staked instead of bent or twisted or flapped as in other cases.

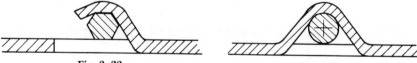

Fig. 2–22.   Fig. 2–23.

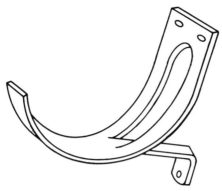

Fig. 2-24.

For successful brazing, large contacting surface areas must exist between the parts to be joined. Therefore, it is always preferable to provide extruded holes in the sheet metal components if the stock is light. In case of prismatic rods, extruded holes are not practical; so in such cases simple or double lancing may be used.

Metal stampings employed as inserts for plastic moldings, die castings, concrete floors, etc., or those which must be embedded in rubber parts, ceramic moldings, etc., must be properly anchored to prevent them from being easily pulled out. A very simple solution for this task is an ordinary, 90 degree lanced tab; greater strength is achieved with two tabs (see Fig. 2-25).

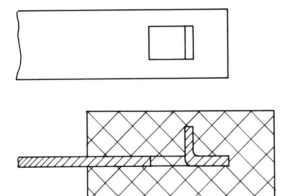

Fig. 2-25.

If the metal stamping is not totally embedded in the plastic molding, but forms one of the outer surfaces of the assembly, then the tabs must be inclined in order to resist both transverse and longitudinal pulls (see Figs. 2-26 and 2-27).

The bulbs of automotive lights are always designed for what is called a "bayonet-lock" joint with the lamp holder. In most instances, the bulb has its joining projections created by lancing as shown in Fig. 2-28. Also, the same design is often found (see Fig. 2-29) in caps or lids used for small containers.

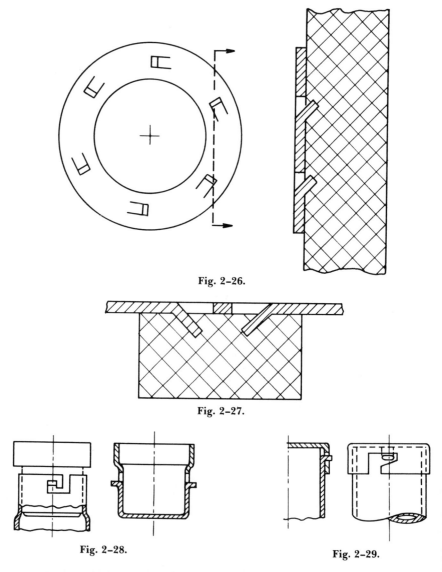

Fig. 2–26.

Fig. 2–27.

Fig. 2–28.   Fig. 2–29.

Tabs are sometimes employed in the temporary fastening of shelves. Such Z-shaped tabs work in combination with matching slots punched in the counterparts (see Fig. 2–30). For similar examples see Boltless Shelving below.

Alignment

For defining the relative positions of two or more parts of which at least one must be a sheet metal component, and where accuracy requirements are of limited importance, one tab is sufficient (see Fig. 2–31). When greater precision is required, two tabs must be foreseen for aligning a sheet metal part with another workpiece (see Fig. 2–32).

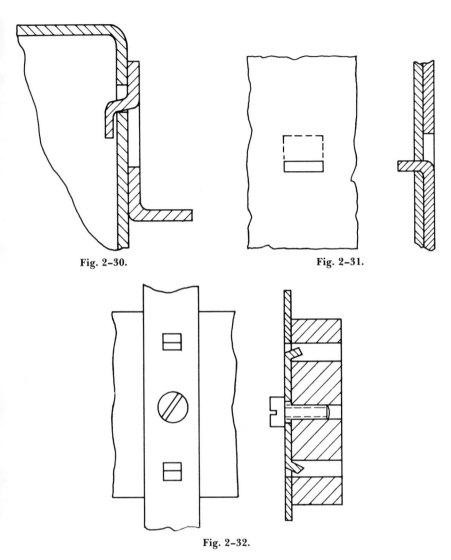

Fig. 2-30.   Fig. 2-31.

Fig. 2-32.

The aligning may be combined with fastening, e.g., lapping. However, it is customary to use stronger fastening means or methods, allowing the lanced tabs to perform the function of alignment and relieving stress, i.e., to avoid lateral loads to the fastening means (riveting, spot welding, flanging, etc.) (see Fig. 2-33).

When accuracy and stress forces are not a primary concern, a few lanced tabs may be designed for guiding a sliding machine member (see Fig. 2-34). For light duty, lanced flaps are used successfully as stops for limiting the travel of pivoting or sliding instruments or machine components (see Fig. 2-35).

Brackets

Single tabs are designed for holding other stationary components, e.g., coils in relays or the hammer in electric bells. For other examples see Fig. 2-36.

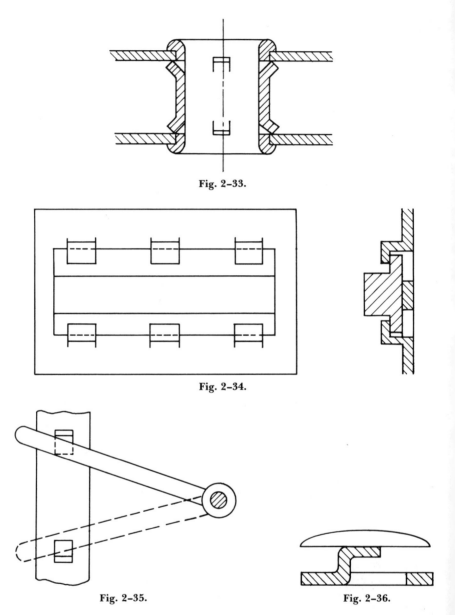

Fig. 2–33.

Fig. 2–34.

Fig. 2–35.   Fig. 2–36.

Boltless Shelving

For assembly of racks without the use of ordinary fasteners, lanced tabs are sometimes used. The simplest design consists of shear-formed and further shaped flaps, formed directly from the vertical posts (see Fig. 2–37). The shelves are then located on the tabs. Other more elaborated designs may be found in some similar commercial products.

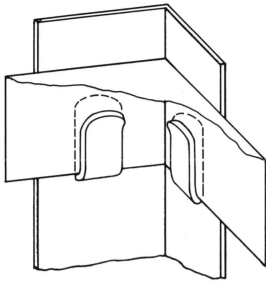

Fig. 2–37.

Miscellaneous

Spacers are easily formed by lancing (see Fig. 2–36). Tote boxes are available with lanced bottoms for easily draining the cutting oils and coolants from machined parts and stampings.

Light duty sprockets may be made by forming evenly spaced tabs in a sheet metal strip, then rolling it into a ring, i.e., at the periphery of a disc which, if necessary, receives a central hub (see Fig. 2–38).

There are several designs of spring-slip connectors where the electrical wire end is held by elastic pressure against a curved, lanced tab. Fig. 2–39 illustrates such a design.

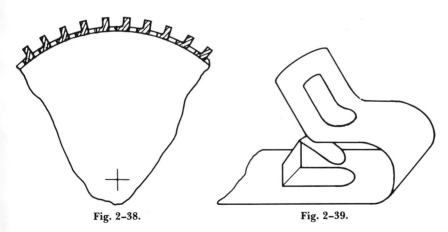

Fig. 2–38.   Fig. 2–39.

Blades for light duty fans are sometimes made in the form of lanced tabs (see Fig. 2–40). Blades for blower wheels are sometimes made in the form of louvered openings.

Z-shaped, lanced lips are formed in steel panels for use in refining petroleum. Staggered inclined lanced tabs with rounded ends are utilized in steel plates employed in machines for threshing, separating, and cleaning grains. They are also used for corncrib siding. In the well-known punch-type can opener, a lanced tab aids in the performance of the device. In book ends, the tab is straight and the parent metal is bent squarely (see Fig. 2–41).

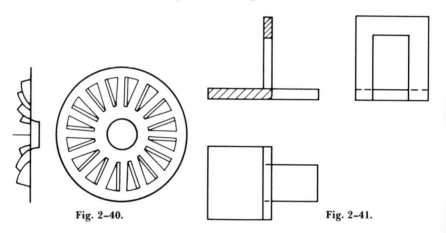

Fig. 2–40.   **Fig. 2–41.**

EMBOSSED SHALLOW RECESSES IN THIN METAL SHEETS

Although widely known and quite often practiced, the embossing of circular protuberances or indentations in the middle of metal sheets (see Fig. 2–42) has not been thoroughly investigated. Research of this subject leads to the following conclusions.

Determining Factors

The maximum depth to which a circular protuberance such as an indentation, recess, boss, dimple, or bulge may be embossed depends on several independent yet partly interdependent factors such as: (1) cross-sectional shape of the boss, (2) both internal and external rounding radii, (3) boss dimensions, (4) stock gage, (5) physical properties of the stock (chiefly stretching factor), (6) boss

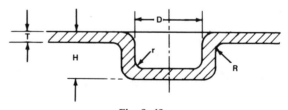

Fig. 2–42.

forming process, (7) location of the boss on the metal sheet, (8) allowable stock thinning, and (9) loads and stresses to which the workpiece will be subjected.

Cross-Sectional Shape

Embossing is a process in which metal flow is produced by stretching. Consequently, the smoother the vertical contour of the boss, the easier the operation and therefore, other conditions being equal, the deeper the boss that may be formed. A large-radius bulge (see Fig. 2–43) is best of all, because this condition allows uniform strain distribution all over the boss (no strain concentrations). Next comes the tapered shape (see Fig. 2–44). This means somewhat less length; however, the stretch around the sharp point is more intense. Tapered shape with a flat bottom having a side inclination at least 15 degrees per side (see Fig. 2–45) is less favorable because at the flat bottom no stretching occurs; all the stretching is concentrated in the tapered walls. The worse design is that of cylindrical walls with a flat bottom as illustrated in Fig. 2–42. This shape has all the drawbacks.

Additionally, the horizontal shape of the boss has a certain influence upon the ease or difficulty of embossing. As in the drawing operation, embossing is better with a circular bulge contour than an elliptical one. And the latter is easier to work with than an elongated bead.

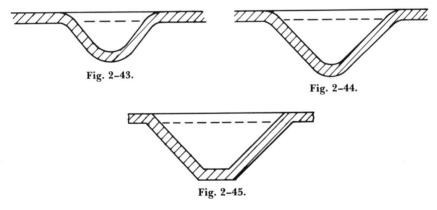

Fig. 2–43.

Fig. 2–44.

Fig. 2–45.

Rounding Radii

For the best results, the rounding radii on both the inside and outside (R and r in Fig. 2–42) should be at least equal to the thickness of the material; it is even more advantageous if the rounding radius is $1\frac{1}{2}$ to 2 times the material thickness.

Boss Diameter

The larger the boss diameter, the greater the allowable depth to which a dimple can be embossed.

Nature of Stock

Since the embossing of small protuberances is a stretching operation, this means thinning out the stock. Therefore, the embossing operation depends largely on the ductility limit of the stock. Of course, for safety reasons, the actual embossing must be stopped well before the ductility limit is reached. The ductility limit varies with the kind and type of metal and alloy in question. The metals are listed below in a decreasing order of ductility as established by S. F. Erichsen, the inventor of the sheet metal ductility testing machine.

1) Brass, deep drawing quality
2) Brass, commercial quality
3) Nickel
4) Copper
5) Steel, deep drawing quality
6) Aluminum
7) Steel, commercial quality
8) Zinc

Forming Process

When using rubber forming dies, the bulge may be created either by an internal or external method. Internally, the rubber must actually push the metal into the female stamp cavity. Externally, the metal is stretched around a protruding metal insert. Since in the latter case more stock surface takes part in the operation, a greater depth can be obtained. If all-metal dies are used, the depth that can be achieved is an intermediate value between the two above cases.

Further improvements may be obtained by forming the bulge in two operations. First, a large diameter, shallow depression is formed, and then it is reduced in diameter and increased in depth. In case of flat bottomed recesses, the two-operation procedure is performed in this way: first, the center of the bottom is stretched, and then the lateral walls are gradually expanded.

Location of Bosses

In order to ensure that a boss will be formed entirely by stretching, it is necessary to locate it well away from the sheet or stamping edge. It is safe practice to leave a distance of at least $2\frac{1}{2}$ to 3 times the stock thickness between the boss edge and sheet edge. Approximately the same distance is also necessary between boss edge and the nearest hole or slot edge.

Stock Thinning

It must be remembered that bulges have thinner walls than the original stock thickness. This is due to the bulges being formed by stretching the metal.

Practical Bulge Depth Limits

Beforehand, it is practically impossible to figure out what limits are possible when forming the depth of a given recess. This depends on so many factors, and many of these factors are uncontrollable. Therefore, it is indispensable to make exhaustive practical trials to determine the best conditions for each case. In many instances it is also necessary to take into account the stresses (loads) which will act upon the stampings afterwards. Thus, overloading that causes failure of components when in service is avoided.

To start practical trials in the case of spherical bulges (see Fig. 2–46), the curve shown in Fig. 2–47 can be successfully used.

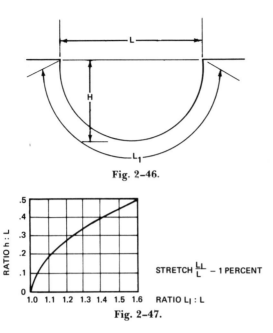

Fig. 2-46.

STRETCH $\dfrac{L_1 L}{L}$ – 1 PERCENT

Fig. 2-47.

Also, the stock thickness should be taken into consideration, e.g., in case of small diameter recesses ($D:T = 10$ to 15) the boss depth should not exceed three times stock thickness. However, as the diameter to thickness ratio increases, the recess depth to thickness ratio may be also augmented. For example, in a .036 in. thick sheet, a flat bottomed recess of 5.25 in. diam (3.375 in diam at the bottom) can be formed to a depth of .906 in. (25 times the stock thickness).

PROTRUSIONS

In the production of sheet metal components for light machinery, tools, devices, and instruments, substantial cost reductions may be realized with protrusions or extruded dowels. Protrusions are also referred to as *partial extrusions, rivet lug forming, partial punching, retained slug forming,* or *semi-perf.* These protrusions are projections (bosses, studs, lugs, plugs, pins, nubs, etc.) integral with the sheet metal or stamping forced out from the flat plane of the metal sheet, on one side or on both sides of the material. They may serve several interesting, important purposes such as: alignment, locating, fastening, separating, pivots, stops, and anchorage for inserts.

Alignment

Ordinary dowel pins always insure accurate alignment, and prevent any alteration in the relative positions in an assembly of two or more stampings. It is quite possible, however, to substitute extra, separate dowel pins by protrusions. The possibilities for such design arrangements are numberless.

The simplest design consists of providing one screw for fastening; the same screw helps the aligning under moderately accurate conditions, and one protrusion matches a punched or drilled hole in the counterpart with a slip fit. For greater accuracy, two protrusions are provided (see Fig. 2–48). The greater the distance between them, the higher the accuracy of the alignment. Sometimes the holes in the counterparts are made blind instead of through holes.

Large panels sometimes use multiple protrusions which are then arranged in the most convenient way, always with as much distance as possible between them. The protrusions serve another function, too. They relieve the fastening screws from lateral or shearing stresses.

In certain instances such as contacts for magnetic contactors, some components must be made adjustable in order to compensate for wear, while still maintaining alignment longitudinally. In such cases, the holes in the counterpart are made elongated.

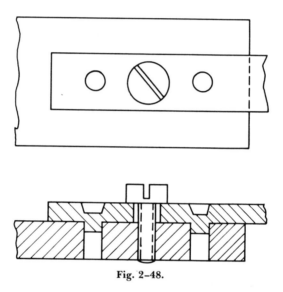

Fig. 2–48.

In another example, two sheet metal components must be held temporarily in perfect location to each other while they are assembled permanently by spot welding. Two protrusions with matching holes in the counterparts are used to temporarily hold the two components in position. In this way, the need for special jigs or fixtures is avoided.

Fastening

Utilizing protrusions as rivets for forming permanent unions is one of the most widely used applications for fastening. Fig. 2–49 shows a typical case where a flat contact spring is fastened to a holder. This method of employing extruded bosses for riveting purposes has a few limitations however. This method can be

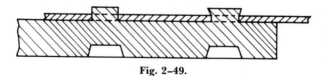

Fig. 2–49.

used only with comparatively thick stock, not less than .100 in. The counterpart sheet (or stamping) must be much thinner than the stud-carrying stamping (never more than half as thick as the stamping with the extruded boss) because the length of the boss is generally limited to a fraction of the stock thickness (see below).

In addition, the assembly cannot resist great loads nor great stresses. In fact, because of the shortness of the stud, there is not sufficient metal to make a regular rivet head. Only a little spreading or flattening can be done (see Fig. 2–49).

Finally, for obvious reasons of economical convenience, such riveting should be used only in mass production jobs, where the building of the dies needed for the operation are justified. (This condition is also valid for all the other applications.)

To perform the riveting operation, it is absolutely necessary to provide a proper anvil (see Fig. 2–50) which supports the bottom of the lug or counter-depression to avoid pressing the lug back into the workpiece.

When two sheet metal parts must be spot welded, both components should be the same thickness. If too great a difference in gages exists, the thinner material will probably become distorted during the welding. For avoiding this trouble, projection welding is recommended. For this purpose, proper protrusions are formed in the thicker material (see Fig. 2–51).

Separating

For fixing a certain, short distance between two stationary or movable stampings, protrusions serve as excellent spacers (see Fig. 2–52). Where sliding mem-

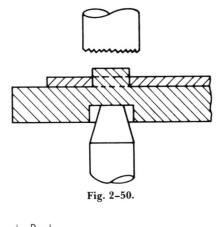

Fig. 2–50.

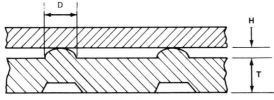

Fig. 2–51.

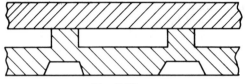

Fig. 2-52.

bers are used over cams or locks, the extruded lugs decrease the contacting surfaces, thus insuring smoother motions. Such applications may be found in adding machines or similar mechanisms.

Pivoting

In some cases, extruded lugs serve for receiving some other member which must operate upon a pivot and also turn around the pivot.

Stops

For limiting the angular or linear movement of a swinging and/or sliding component, protrusions may be used sometimes in the counterpart. Fig. 2-53 illustrates an example where extruded bosses are utilized both for stops and as a pivot.

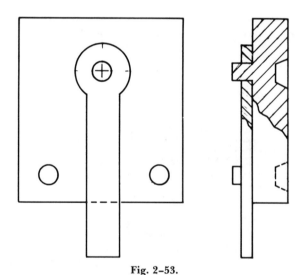

Fig. 2-53.

Anchorage for Inserts

Sheet metal inserts must be firmly anchored in the main workpieces so that they cannot be pulled out of the plastic moldings or die castings. Sometimes protrusions are used for this purpose as illustrated in Fig. 2-54.

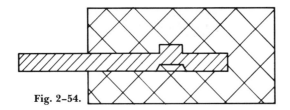

Fig. 2-54.

Forming Protrusions

Extruded bosses may be formed in several ways. Almost all of the corresponding methods employ comparatively simple, and therefore, inexpensive press tools. There are three basic tool design types:
1) Standard punching die
2) Standard die plate and special (enlarged) punch
3) Special die plate and special punch.

Of course, the above mentioned tools may be employed not only in case of separate second operation punching tools but also in a preliminary station of progressive dies. Probably the latter is more frequent than the former. The same methods are employed also for the formation of blind holes in the counterparts for receiving protrusions. Only one-diameter, cylindrical punch ends are employed for this purpose.

Protrusions are often confused with embossed dimples (see Figs. 2–42 through 2–45). There is a basic difference between these two design details. In embossing, there is a stretching which causes some stock thinning. In protrusion forming, there is a metal displacement very closely related to coining. Also, the shapes are different. Embossed dimples are always streamlined and well-rounded, while protrusions have rather square, sharp corners.

The cross section of the extruded bosses is generally round to achieve low-cost tooling. However, sometimes they are made oval, oblong, square, rectangular, round with a flat side, polygonal, or irregular in some other ways. Such special shapes are used to avoid the possibility of turning the workpiece around for radial alignment or to match mating holes in counterparts.

Of course, for protrusions, punch-penetration must be made shorter than the data given in Table II–I. On the other hand, the minimum penetration must be sufficient so that the punch passes the elastic limit of the stock. Otherwise no permanent deformation of the metal will occur. This is analogous to what happens in bending. A bending radius must be small enough to create permanent deformation.

Standard Punching Die. A standard punching die is used by limiting the descent of the punch and thereby arresting the punch-penetration into the metal before the slug is actually severed from it (see Fig. 2–55). This method only allows comparatively short boss heights because, on the heavy gage metals used for protrusions, the slug severs with a minimum amount of penetration. Penetration of the punch depends on the following factors:
1) Nature of the metal. If the metal is less ductile, there is less penetration.
2) Stock hardness. If the metal is harder, there is less penetration.

**Table II-1. Necessary Punch Penetration for
Severing a Low Carbon Steel Slug.**

Sheet Metal Thickness (In.)	Punch-Penetration Compared to Thickness of Material (Percent)
$1/32$	87
$1/16$	75
$3/32$	67
$1/8$	62
$3/16$	56
$1/4$	50
$5/16$	47
$3/8$	44
$1/2$	37
$5/8$	34
$3/4$	31
1	25

3) Thickness. If the gage of the metal is heavier, there is less penetration.
4) Punch clearance. If the punch has a smaller clearance, there is greater penetration.
5) D/t ratio. If the ratio is smaller, there is greater penetration.
6) Sharpness of cutting edges. If the edges are dull, there is greater penetration.

A guide to necessary punch penetration for mild, low-carbon steel, is given in Table II-1.

Special Punch and Standard Die Plate. To obtain greater boss heights and to avoid the danger of unintentional slug severance, the first step consists of substituting a tool having an upward tapered shape (see Fig. 2-56) for the standard punch of the preceding tool (see Fig. 2-55).

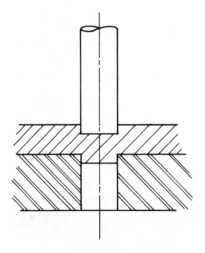

Fig. 2-55.

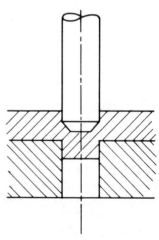

Fig. 2-56.

The second step consists of enlarging the punch (straight or tapered) about 25 percent above the hole diameter value (see Fig. 2–57) thus getting larger boss heights. This design is employed usually with light gage stock, and where the length of the boss does not exceed half of the boss diameter.

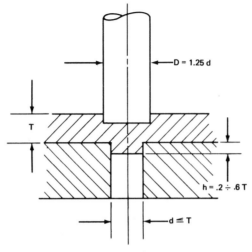

Fig. 2–57.

Further improvements are obtained by making stepped punches (see Fig. 2–58). These have two portions: the point is smaller in diameter than the boss diameter, and a top section has a larger diameter than the boss diameter. This design is preferred with heavy gage material, and where the length of the extruded boss is higher than half of its diameter. The point is sometimes tapered and in other cases curved (with a radius $R = D/2$).

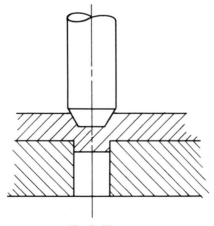

Fig. 2–58.

Though a standard die opening shape with the side relief downward is satisfactory, it is preferable to use one with straight cylindrical walls, and it is even better if these walls are tapered slightly downward. Thus, the ejection of the finished workpieces is facilitated.

In all these cases, a restricted flow into the adjacent metal and an unrestricted flow into the die opening occur. This is why comparatively high bosses of great strength are swaged out.

Closed Die Plates. Some tool designers prefer closed bottom die openings, or die openings provided with backing up pins combined with ejectors (Fig. 2–59). Supposedly, such tools produce more compact lugs or bosses with greater strength. In such cases, the punch is practically always of an enlarged size of greater diameter than the hole.

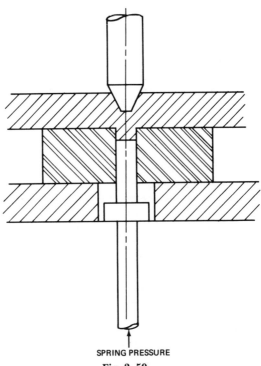

SPRING PRESSURE

Fig. 2–59.

special considerations

Since the major cost in metal stampings is the cost of the material, any efforts during the design stage of any component to minimize scrap may result in substantial savings. Other considerations involve obtaining additional strength from the material by using reinforcing processes such as flanging, ribs, corrugations, etc., to best advantage. Close attention to the possibility of stacking certain types of blanks and attention to their assembly by choosing the appropriate assembly method may result in further savings.

DESIGNING FOR MINIMUM SCRAP

Sound practice in designing circular components or high production parts can save material by modifying the part and yet, at the same time, strive to preserve part strength or to further strengthen it.

Circular Components

If blanked in a straight row, circular components have a low material utilization factor. The material is utilized to a greater advantage if a wider strip of material is selected, and the workpieces blanked in more than one row in a staggered form on the strip.

In case of large rings, material waste can be reduced by designing the rings in a composite construction (see Figs. 3–1 and 3–2). After blanking them in two or more segments, they are assembled and welded, or they may be joined by other suitable means.

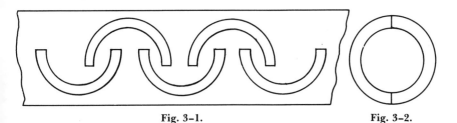

Fig. 3–1.   Fig. 3–2.

In addition, the designer should explore the possibilities of flat-forming (edge-forming) a piece of a bar into a ring and welding the joint (see Fig. 3–3).

45

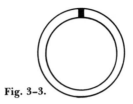

Fig. 3–3.

High-Production, Scrapless Design of Stampings

As suggested above, the most functional detail in many metal stampings is the hole pattern. The outer contour or shape of the stamping is, in such cases, practically immaterial.

Sound practice takes advantage of such conditions to achieve several economical and technical advantages. In fact, by slight or substantial modifications of the outer contour of blanks, it is easy to obtain a scrapless design. This means substantial savings in raw material, simplification (and cost saving) of tooling, and often drastically increased production output. In the majority of cases, it is additionally advantageous to produce two workpieces at each press hit. In such fashion, the labor cost has been decreased by as much as 50 percent.

Case histories in which all the above advantages have been realized are presented in this chapter. The first example clearly illustrates the underlying principles. The part designed originally as per Fig. 3–4 needed $1.70 \times .52 =$

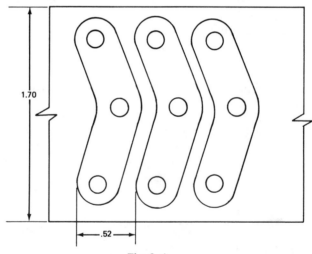

Fig. 3–4.

.884 sq in. stock surface. The part was redesigned as shown in Fig. 3–5. The three holes of identical dimensions as before are located at the same center distances and at the same distances from the stamping edge. The new stamping is actually stronger than the original one; it has more surface and more mass. The scrapless stamping needs only $1.56 \times .45 = .702$ sq in. surface, saving .182 sq in. (a 20 percent material savings). The stamping outer contours shown in

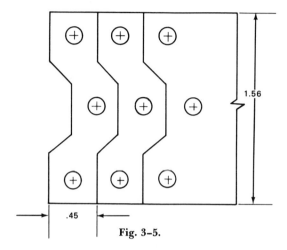

Fig. 3-5.

Fig. 3–6 and 3–7 are more substantial, and the function of the part is not impaired at all.

The next case is a typical example of scrapless design through an intermediary step. Fig. 3–8 illustrates the original design and corresponding strip layout. Fig. 3–9 shows a semiscrapless design which is already a notable improvement over the original design. However, the best design is the totally scrapless one portrayed in Fig. 3–10. Blanking is always performed in the same direction.

The inline arrangement of the stampings (as presented in the examples

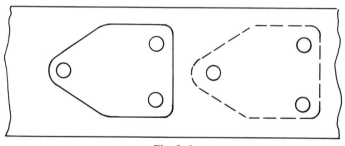

Fig. 3-6.

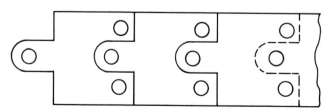

Fig. 3-7.

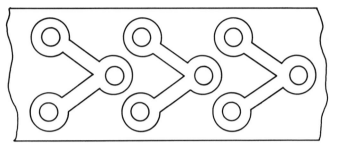

Fig. 3–8.

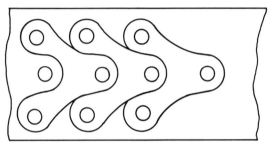

Fig. 3–9.

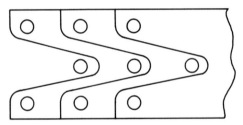

Fig. 3–10.

of Figs. 3–4 through 3–10) is not always possible. In many instances, the stamp-ings must be arranged in the strip in such a way that they are stamped in an alternately reversed manner. The second blank, which is produced simul-taneously, is oriented at 180 deg with respect to the blanking punch shape. Figs. 3–11 and 3–12 illustrate this alternately reversing principle with a simple triangular stamping. Figs. 3–13 through 3–15 again illustrate a solution which contemplates an intermediary step to reach the totally scrapless design solution. Fig. 3–16 shows a transformer lamination with a totally scrapless design which produces two parts at each press hit. Sometimes quite intricate shapes are com-bined into a scrapless design. This is obtained through interlocking, jigsaw puzzle-like arrangements (see Figs. 3–17 and 3–18).

Up to this point, stampings with predominantly straight contour lines have been dealt with — at least the modified shapes are formed by straight lines. Scrap-

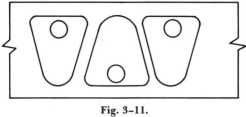

Fig. 3–11.

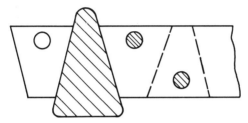

Fig. 3–12.

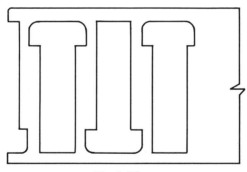

Fig. 3–13.

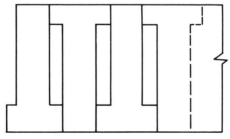

Fig. 3–14.

less design is also used quite frequently with curved outer contours. Figs. 3–19 and 3–20 illustrate typical cases in which a little side notching is included that also serves as an excellent "french" stop.

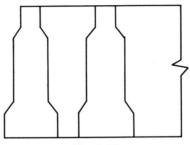

Fig. 3–15.

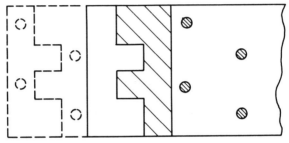

Fig. 3–16.

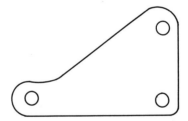

Fig. 3–17.

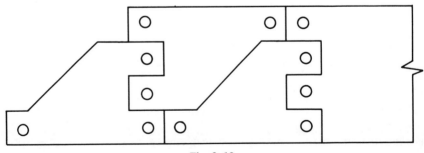

Fig. 3–18.

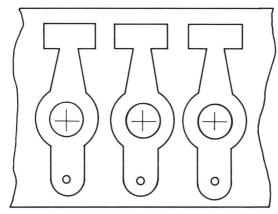

Fig. 3–19.

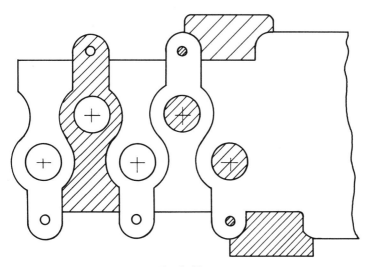

Fig. 3–20.

Sometimes the double-blanking scrapless die instead of producing two identical stampings at each press hit, produces two different stampings at each press stroke. In these cases, the stampings and the tools are usually so designed that the punched slugs are bona fide stampings. Figs. 3–21 through 3–23 illustrate typical examples. Figs. 3–24 and 3–25 show a lucky case where the original blank almost without any modification allowed a high-production scrapless design along with all the advantages offered by this kind of stamping production.

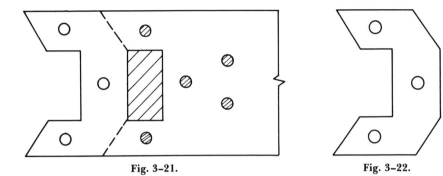

Fig. 3-21.

Fig. 3-22.

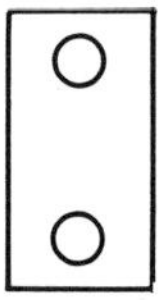

Fig. 3-23.

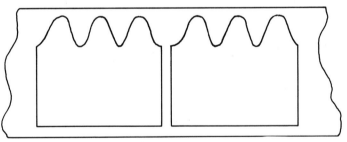

Fig. 3-24.

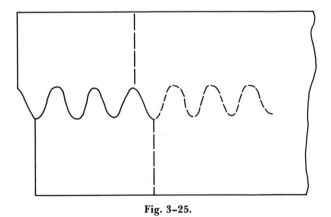

Fig. 3-25.

REINFORCING PROCESSES

Two of the chief advantages of sheet metal stampings are their relatively low cost and light weight. To effectively utilize these advantages, some reinforcing detail must, at times, be considered. This makes the stamping structurally stronger, more resistant to specific loads, with little or no significant increase in weight. Several press working methods by which stampings may be reinforced are: bending, curling, hemming, seaming, and rib-forming.

Metal stampings are not usually calculated for strength; they are only designed for convenient production and correct performance. Their dimensions are determined empirically, depending on the function of the component and personal judgment and experience of personnel involved in the design of the stampings. At any rate, testing samples to establish the design before beginning actual production always gives a good control of the design. However, there are cases of highly stressed stampings which may break down during these testing processes because of insufficient strength. In such instances, they must be checked for resistance and reinforced accordingly.

Weak stampings may be strengthened by employing stronger material, by employing the same material with a heavier gage, or by using a lighter gage material that is structurally reinforced. The chief cost factor is the raw material employed for production. Since in the majority of cases it is more convenient to use thinner stock of commercial quality, it is usually more convenient to use a reinforcing method.

This chapter discusses only two kinds of loads: bending or flection, and buckling, which are the types of loads that metal stampings are more likely to encounter.

Strength of materials teaches that in case of a cantilever beam stressed with a load concentrated at the free end for bending (see Fig. 3–26), the deflection, f, is:

$$f = \frac{PL^3}{3EI} \tag{3-1}$$

Where: P = load (lbs)
L = free length of unsupported beam (in.)
E = modulus of elasticity (lbs/sq in.)
I = moment of inertia (in^4)

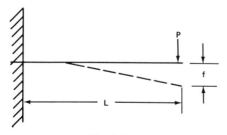

Fig. 3–26.

This means that in case of a component having a given length L, made from a certain material E, and subjected to a determined load P, the deflection f is inversely proportional to the moment of inertia I.

The latter depends only on the cross-sectional shape of the component, and precisely on the form and dimensions of the cross section. If the beam corresponds to any other design such as simple, or mixed beam, with the load distributed or concentrated at any point, the deflection is always inversely proportional to the moment of inertia.

The buckling strength of an object is checked with the well known Euler's equation:

$$P = \frac{C\pi^2 IE}{L^2}$$ (3–2)

Where: P = total ultimate safe load (lbs)
C = safety factor
I = moment of inertia (in^4)
E = modulus of elasticity of material (lbs/sq in.)
L = length of column (in.)

Eq. 3-2 shows that if a component has a given length L and is made from a certain material E, the maximum load depends directly on the moment of inertia.

Consequently, in both bending and buckling the strength improvement must be concerned with the moment of inertia. Therefore, how will the strength and the moment of inertia of stampings change with the application of reinforcing elements?

Flanging

From actual practice, the following results are obtainable. Given a component made from plane, flat stock with a width of 2 in. and a thickness of .100 in. (see Fig. 3–27), the moment of inertia, calculated with the basic equation, is:

$$I = bd^3 \div 12$$ (3–3)
$$I = 2 \times .100^3 \div 12 = .000167 \text{ in}^4$$

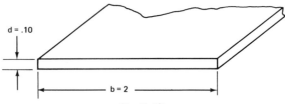

d = .10

b = 2

Fig. 3–27.

Although a one-sided flange will add considerable strength, two-sided flanges (channel type work) are preferred because such a design allows better load distribution conditions. The smallest admissible height of flanges is about two times the material thickness (see Fig. 3-28). If this value is used, the moment of inertia is:

$$I = .0011 \text{ in}^4$$

This corresponds to an increase in resistance or strength in relation to Fig. 3-27 of about 5.6 times, while the material employed has been increased only by 20 percent (from .20 in² to .24 in²).

With an increase in the leg height, the moment of inertia increases considerably. In Figs. 3-28 through 3-32 a few designs in progressive order of

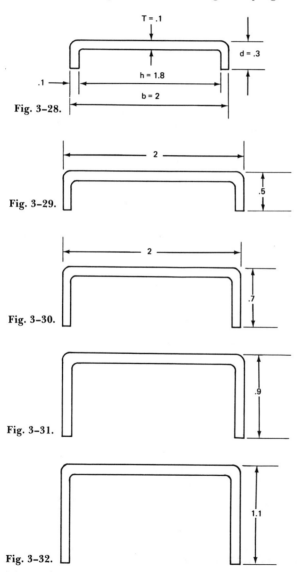

Fig. 3-28.

Fig. 3-29.

Fig. 3-30.

Fig. 3-31.

Fig. 3-32.

flange height are shown, and Table III-1 gives the corresponding calculated values.

Table III-1.   Calculated Strength Values for Flanged Stampings.

Fig. No.	Area Sq In.	Increase of Area to Fig. 3-27 (Percent)	Moment of Inertia	Increase of Moment of Inertia to Fig. 3-27 in Percent
3-27	.20	—	.000167	—
3-28	.24	20	.0011	.560
3-29	.28	40	.0062	3.600
3-30	.32	60	.0162	9.600
3-31	.36	80	.0278	16.560
3-32	.40	100	.0500	29.900

Combined Shapes

For elementary shaped sections (rectangular, square, circular, channel, L, etc.), the moment of inertia about an axis passing through its center of gravity is easily found in any engineering handbook, or manufacturer's catalog. For combined shapes, the designer must calculate the moment of inertia for the whole system. The results for a few typical shapes follow.

Joggling

The first practical case is illustrated in Fig. 3-38.

$$I = .00213 \text{ in}^4$$

In this case an increase of 16.7 percent in area (with respect to Fig. 3-28) brought an increase in strength of almost 100 percent. However, a comparison of the values in Fig. 3-33 with those of Fig. 3-29, whose cross-sectional

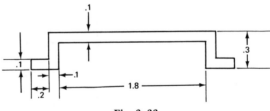

Fig. 3-33.

area is the same, will reveal that there is an increase in strength of the last shape of almost 300 percent. The simple explanation of this phenomenon lies in the basic formula of a rectangular shape (see Eq. 3-3): while the moment of inertia is directly proportional to the breadth, it is directly proportional to the third power of the height.

Compound Bends

Since the moment of inertia takes into account only one axis around which are grouped the various portions of a given section, it does not matter in which direction the different legs of a formed workpiece are bent as long as the legs are parallel to the neutral axis. Consequently, the workpiece in Fig. 3–34 must be treated exactly as the component in Fig. 3–33. Thus, the moment of inertia is the same in both cases.

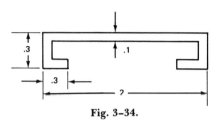

Fig. 3–34.

Ribs

The area of the cross section illustrated in Fig. 3–35 is .2185 sq in. The calculated moment of inertia is:

$$I = .00124 \text{ in}^4$$

A comparison of Fig. 3–35 with Fig. 3–28 will reveal the following interesting results: with about a 10 percent decrease in material with respect to Fig. 3–28, an increase in strength of about 10 percent is realized.

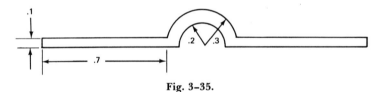

Fig. 3–35.

For reasons explained with reference to compound bends (see Fig. 3–34), the position of the rib with respect to the symmetrical axis or any axis perpendicular to the neutral axis is immaterial. So, the shapes in Figs. 3–36 and 3–37

Fig. 3–36.   Fig. 3–37.

have the same moment of inertia values as that of Fig. 3–35 as long as the corresponding values of breadth, radii, stock thickness, etc. remain the same.

If the center of the cross-sectional figure is occupied functionally, then it is preferable to design two lateral ribs (see Fig. 3–38). In this case, the moment of inertia is:

$$I = .0019412 \text{ in}^4$$

A comparison of the results of Figs. 3–35 and 3–38 reveals that another increase of about 9 percent in material (from a .2185 to a .237 sq in. area) increased the strength by more than 50 percent.

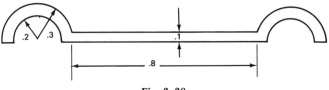

Fig. 3–38.

Ribs are often of the closed type, running entirely in the panel of the metal sheet. Since these ribs are formed by stretching the metal, there is a rather low limit to the possibilities of forming such ribs, and the value of height is limited. However, in case of open type ribs where the ends of the bead are open, the rib height is unlimited because these ribs are formed by bending. In these instances, the component strength is increased considerably by the addition of small quantities of metal as illustrated in Fig. 3–39 whose moment of inertia is:

$$I = .003697 \text{ in}^4$$

A comparison of Fig. 3–39 with Fig. 3–35 reveals that a slight increase in area of less than 20 percent (from .2185 to .2585 sq in.) increased the strength of the workpiece by approximately 200 percent.

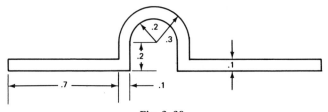

Fig. 3–39.

In the case of closed ribs up to certain reasonable limits, it is not necessary to take into account the decrease of material thickness due to stretching. Actual tests have shown that the hardening due to cold working provides an increase in tensile strength which more than compensates for the thinning of the stock.

Corrugated Panels

The cross-sectional shape of corrugated sheets may be considered, for all practical purposes, as an uninterrupted series of corrugated ribs (see Fig. 3–40). The corresponding moment of inertia values depend upon the material thick-

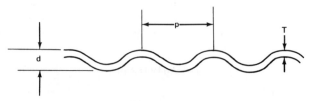

Fig. 3–40.

ness T, mean depth d, projected width under consideration b, and the ratio between pitch p and depth. In their catalogs, the manufacturers of such goods give the corresponding calculated moment of inertia values, or at least the equations by which they may be easily calculated.

For example, the Aluminum Company of America gives the following simple empirical equation in its *Alcoa Structural Handbook* (1):

$$I = kbTd^2 \qquad\qquad (3\text{-}4)$$

Where: $k = .15$ in case of $p/d = 3$
$k = .13$ in case of $p/d = 5$

Examination of one of Alcoa's standard types (Industrial Roofing and Siding sheet) results in the following actual data:

$$p = 2.67$$
$$d = .875$$
$$T = .032$$
$$I = .0409 \text{ in}^4/\text{ft width}$$

Area of the cross section $= .469$ in^2

A comparison of the above corrugated panel with a flat panel yields the following facts:

1) Taking a panel of the same width (12 in.) and the same thickness (.032 in.), and multiplying $= 12 \times .032 = .384$ in^2. This is about 20 percent less than that of the corrugated sheet. On the other hand, the moment of inertia of this flat sheet is $I = 12 \times .032^3 \div 12 = .000032768$ in^4. The strength becomes about $1/1250$ of that of the corrugated sheet.

2) Taking the same original corrugated sheet and flattening it results in a flat sheet about 15 in. wide. The moment of inertia of this panel becomes $I = 15 \times .032^3 \div 12 = .00004086$ in^4. The strength becomes about $\frac{1}{1000}$ of that of the original corrugated panel.

Curling

Curling may be formed only at the ends of flat workpieces. The cross-sectional area is simply divided into two hollow circles or tubes and a rectangular portion located tangentially to the two rings (see Fig. 3-41). In a practical

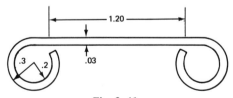

Fig. 3-41.

example, a rather thin gage value of .03 in. has been chosen to calculate the moment of inertia because it is not customary to perform curling operations on comparatively thick stock.

$$I = .003045 \text{ in}^4$$

A comparison with any of the preceding shapes would be misleading, because the thickness of material determines the amount of material stiffness. Therefore, a flanged section has been made up (see Fig. 3–42) of the same sheet gage and dimensions in order to compare the two shapes.

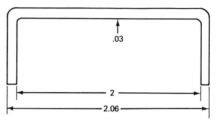

Fig. 3–42.

The moment of inertia of the flanged shape is: $I = .001512 \text{ in}^4$, and its area $A = .087 \text{ in}^2$. Now, comparing these values with those corresponding to the curled shape shown in Fig. 3–41, the following advantages of the latter are apparent: with a metal employment ratio of 4 to 5, there is a strength ratio of about two to one.

Thus, if the radius of the curls is decreased arbitrarily and made to occupy a flat sheet of the same cross-sectional area in both cases (see Fig. 3–43), the new moment of inertia is:

$$I = .0016234 \text{ in}^4$$

This value is almost half as much as the value found for Fig. 3–41, proving that when the radius of a curl is reduced, the moment of inertia is decreased.

Fig. 3–43.

Hemming

The strength of the hemmed sheet is not easy to accurately calculate because hemmed edges should not be entirely closed, yet the strength depends upon how much the hem is closed. Completely closing a hem requires severe cold working of the metal and too great a press tonnage.

Assuming that the hem is completely closed (see Fig. 3–44), and that the two end portions with their rounded edges may be considered as full rectangles with an extremely reduced influence, the approximate value of the moment of inertia is:

$$I = .0000144 \text{ in}^4$$

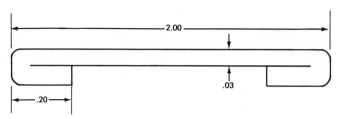

Fig. 3–44.

The moment of inertia of a comparable flat section, 2.00 in. × .030 in., is:

$$I = .000045 \text{ in}^4$$

and area is:

$$A = .060 \text{ in}^2$$

Therefore, an area increase of 20 percent will increase strength 300 percent.

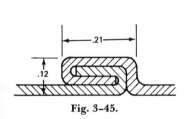

Fig. 3–45.

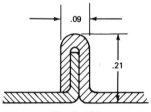

Fig. 3–46.

This means that even if this is less than the increase in flanged shapes (see Fig. 3–28), or even less than the curled shapes, the result is still quite satisfactory.

Seaming

Since the moment of inertia of any section composed of several layers of the same thickness is equal to the third power of the number of layers, the strength of a standard flat seam is proportional to the third power of the number of layers of which it is composed. So, the moment of inertia of the seam presented in Fig. 3–45 is roughly:

$$I = .0000294 \text{ in}^4$$

In the case of vertical seams, the corresponding strength is quite high. In fact, the material is obviously better utilized for strength. As Fig. 3–46 shows, with one layer less which saves one-third of the material, a considerable increase in strength of more than 100 percent is achieved, although the locking ability is sacrificed somewhat.

$$I = .0000695 \text{ in}^4$$

Rigidized Sheets

Embossed sheet metal is currently supplied in a wide variety of patterns for light duty decorative applications. These sheets have greater strength than the original flat sheet from which they are made. This added strength is obtained by correct redistribution or displacement of the metal. In fact, the cross-sectional area at any given point resembles that of corrugated panels. As demonstrated above, such an arrangement increases the strength of a given panel. Of course, the rigidity increase is not spectacular, but it is interesting and useful. Table III–2 illustrates the increase in rigidity proven through actual tests.

Table III–2. Rigidity Increase of Embossed Sheet Metal.

Material	Increase (Percent)
SAE 1010 Carbon Steel:	
Transversal	19.5
Longitudinal	14.2
1.77 Stainless Steel — Full Hard	88.0
24ST Aluminum Alloy	108.0

It should be pointed out that the reinforcing processes provoke internal stresses in the formed zones, and the components are susceptible to larger loads. Therefore, it is very important to check the forming operations to avoid such troubles by making bends with large bending radii, beads with rounded shapes, beads widely spaced, etc.

Sometimes cold working thin stock thins it even more, but the thinning actually increases the tensile strength through work hardening. So, formed sections are usually stronger than straight ones. As a result of the reinforcing processes, strength-to-weight ratio in stampings is decidedly higher than with any other metal working method.

Functions of Formed Ribs

Ribs may be used in several ways for solving design problems. Some usual and special ways that their versatility can be used to advantages are described below.

Ribs can be used to increase the rigidity or bending strength of thin sheet metal parts. If a short, narrow piece of half-hard copper folio of .004 in. thickness (or a piece of ordinary paper) is held at one end, it will bend under its own weight. By forming a simple semicircular or triangular rib in its middle, it becomes rigid enough not only to support itself but also to easily support a load of a couple of ounces.

A small bracket made from sheet metal needs a certain cross section for resisting the specified load. By embossing a corner stiffening rib, the component can be made from the same sheet metal with a saving in cross section of at least 50 percent. Components subjected to buckling loads increase their strength 4 to 8 times by careful application of stiffener ribs (see Fig. 3–47).

In a few applications, ribs or beads help to avoid trouble caused by detrimental forces. Often, metal sheets or sheet metal parts have internal stresses. These may be created by cold working, by heat treatment, or even by prolonged storage. Such internal stresses may be partially or even totally eliminated by careful use of ribs (see Fig. 3–48).

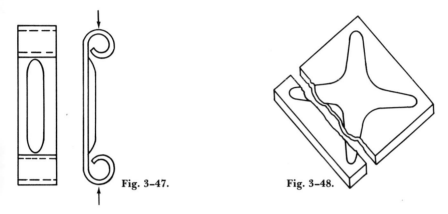

Fig. 3–47.   Fig. 3–48.

Finally, in temporary assemblies with a sliding fit, a proper circular bead functions as a spring-element for supplying the necessary elastic force for the assembly. Beads are extensively used for permanent assembly by crimping (see Chapter 4). Crimped unions may be made in several forms: between two hollow workpieces, inward (Fig. 3–49) or outward, between a tubing and a solid shaft, between a piece of tubing and a disc, between a piece of tubing and a punched sheet metal part, or a drilled flat part.

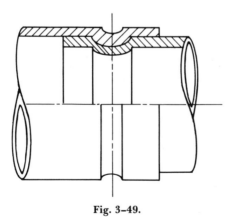

Fig. 3–49.

Projection welding is another kind of permanent joint using rib-like details. In one of the sheet metal parts, usually the thicker one, small embossed protuberances or circular beads are formed which are then utilized for the welding process.

In thin walled round parts such as drawn cups and pieces of tubing, rounded threads are embossed for creating temporary unions (see Fig. 3-50). Typical are electrical bulbs, lampholder sockets, small reflectors for flashlights, and glass closures.

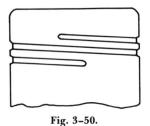

Fig. 3-50.

Sheet metal panels under certain vibration-provoking conditions become noisy. One of the possible remedies is to form certain rib patterns. The frequency of the panel is then changed, and thus, the noise is reduced; it may be even totally eliminated.

In a few instances, embossed ribs are employed for safety. First, the so-called "nonslip" metallic floors for factories, mechanic shops, and garages are made up from sheet metal panels in which certain figures are embossed. Thus, shoes will not slip, even if the floor surfaces are somewhat oily or greasy. Embossed ribs also provide grips on wheels and handles to prevent the operator's hands from slipping (see Fig. 3-51).

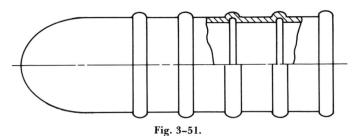

Fig. 3-51.

Spacers create small distances between two workpieces without the need for extra parts. This arrangement is especially convenient if close tolerances are involved in which the raised small contacting surfaces are quickly and easily machined to the required dimensions (see Fig. 3-52).

Beads formed on round parts are excellent means for properly aligning them with other round matching components (see Fig. 3-53). Ribs or dimples embossed in sheet metal parts used as inserts in plastic moldings serve well as anchors (for increasing resistance of the insert against being pulled out of the plastic molding) (see Fig. 3-54).

Ribs and other embossed patterns are used often for ornamental purposes, especially to break the monotony of large panels by enlivening them with embossed figures and pictures. The decorative function may be and often is combined with a practical purpose. The embossed figures may carry some message

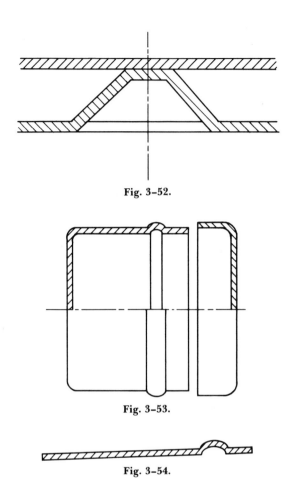

Fig. 3-52.

Fig. 3-53.

Fig. 3-54.

such as a simple advertisement, or a direction about the use of the contents in a can. At the same time, embossed figures or decorative ribs may have functional purposes such as stress-relieving, safety, noise reduction, etc.

STACKED STAMPINGS

Stacked stampings usually allow attractive cost reductions. Additionally, the output of high-speed punch presses means higher production per hour than with the comparatively slow machine tools. When using the stacked stamping technique for making a given part, the first step in designing it consists of establishing the number of layers and their individual thicknesses. This design phase must be a compromise between two opposing principles.

On one hand, thinner stock means a more uniform side surface. This is true because there is less break-surface and the shear-surfaces are better distributed. On the other hand, a higher quantity of layers means more labor, and a more difficult and delicate assembly of the laminations. A convenient thickness for average cases is $\frac{1}{16}$ in. sheet. Of course, it must be changed whenever necessary or advisable.

Assembly Methods

Another important detail in the design of stacked stampings is the selection of the most appropriate assembly method. The blanks constituting a stacked stamping must be properly positioned and secured firmly in their relative positions. No loads, nor stresses of foreseen magnitudes should be able to change the shape and/or dimensions of a stacked stamping. Sometimes the two functions are performed by the same auxiliary member or method. However, quite frequently two separate means for alignment and fastening are used.

For stacked stampings, several possible methods exist, but no one method is actually preferred. The function, size and shape of the part, the characteristics of the material used, the available financial means, the available production equipment, and other details are the determining factors for the selection of the most suitable and convenient method in every individual case.

The blanks should be designed with as few holes as possible. Therefore, it is considered poor practice to design too many extra holes for aligning and fastening. Following the same concept, the best design uses very few extra parts, or none at all.

The least expensive assembly method employs bolts, keys, etc. to join the stacked stampings to the mating parts (see Fig. 3–55). This is a temporary fastening method. In another temporary fastening method, stacks composed of many layers having the same size and shape are held together with cold drawn rods threaded on both ends and provided with matching nuts and washers (see Fig. 3–56).

Among the permanent type fastening methods, pinning is one of the most popular and the most frequently used. In pinning, an adequate number of holes of suitable size and location are punched in the blank. After stacking the layers, groove pins with ridges running parallel to the axis are pressed into these holes. These pins provide excellent alignment of the blanks (see Fig. 3–57).

The drive fit of the pins is often utilized simultaneously for holding together the stack. For cases of low stress and low loads this is an adequate fastening method. For those cases that need a stronger fastening for the stack, either hot riveting or brazing are used in addition to pinning.

A very inexpensive, yet very efficient method consists of putting the assembled stack with the groove pins inserted in their holes between two flat electrodes of a spot welder. Thus, the protruding ends are headed (hot riveted). When the assembly cools, the shrinking pins tightly pull the stock together.

To improve the appearance of the joint, the outer rivet holes are sometimes countersunk. Thus, flush leads are provided. It must be taken into account, however, that this design increases the manufacturing costs considerably. In addition, the fastening is weaker than the one with the exposed rivet heads.

The layers of stacked stampings are frequently brazed together, and if the brazing is properly executed, the results are usually excellent. However, this method is rather expensive. Very important details in this respect are: flatness and cleanliness of the blanks prior to assembly.

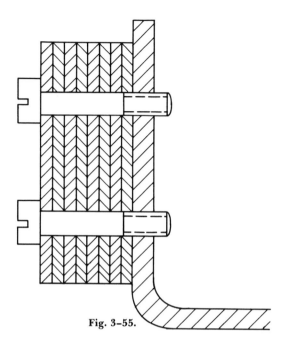

Fig. 3-55.

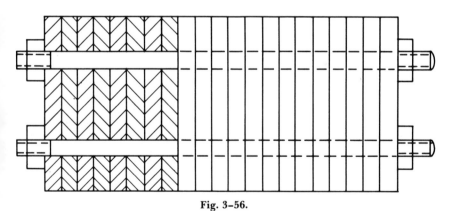

Fig. 3-56.

While the usual standard brazing process for stacked stampings is performed in furnaces, sometimes very good results are obtained with "salt pot" brazing, especially if there are special holes in the stampings for properly locating the brazing slugs (see Fig. 3-58). The use of clad metals such as tin or zinc coated steel sheets greatly facilitates heat assembly methods such as brazing or soldering.

Standard, commercially available rivets for fastening purposes are not recommended. Although they are inexpensive and would be practical since the parts do not have to be so clean and flat as in brazing, riveting body diameter

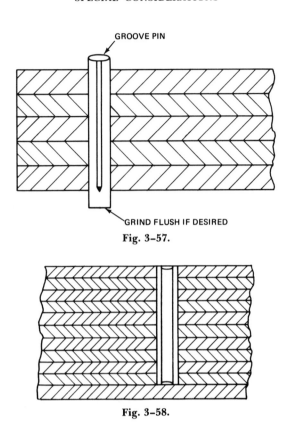

Fig. 3-57.

Fig. 3-58.

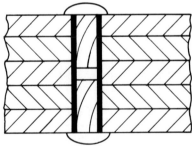

Fig. 3-59.

tolerances are quite wide, so they require holes with loose fits. When higher alignment accuracy is required, screw machine-made rivets are employed.

Hollow, steel, cylindrical roll pins are another means of assembling stacked stampings. These are employed like groove pins, but roll pins create less intensive fits than groove pins. Normally, the protruding ends must be sanded away to get flush surfaces.

If a tighter fit is desired with the use of a roll pin, hardened drive screws are forced in the center of the roll pin from opposite ends (see Fig. 3-59).

Staking and riveting are closely related fastening methods; in both cases, plastic deformation of stock is used for creating permanent mechanical joints. In a sprocket wheel produced as a stacked stamping, the alignment may be made with any adequate means (e.g., pins), and the fastening of both the laminations among themselves and the lamination stack to the central hub is accomplished by means of staking (see Fig. 3–60).

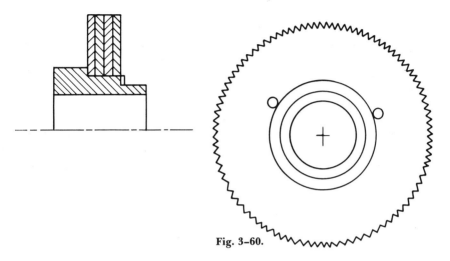

Fig. 3-60.

In some cases, simple drive nails may give satisfactory results for aligning the layers. Of course, some suitable method must be used to fasten together the stack such as brazing, or spot-welding. In some exceptional instances, hollow rivets or short pieces of tubing are successfully employed for alignment and fastening. The fastening power may be increased by proper brazing. The hollow rivet may be threaded, thus adding a third function to the original two; to serve as a nut for fastening the stacked stamping to a mating part (see Fig. 3–61).

Sometimes, if there are no lateral stresses to be taken care of, the alignment is omitted; it is simply the fastening means which keeps the layers in their cor-

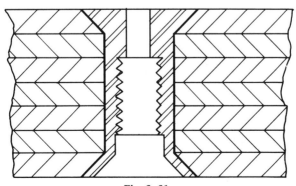

Fig. 3-61.

rect relative position. Such is the case of small brazed stacked stampings made up of a few blanks. Of course, the stack must be clamped together firmly during the brazing process. For this purpose, stainless steel screws, nuts and washers might be used. These have a lower coefficient of thermal expansion than standard low-carbon steel. Thus, the clamping power of the fastening means becomes stronger as the temperature rises.

Spot welding is another popular fastening means which is sometimes used alone without any alignment. If the equipment is available, stacks of $^3/_8$ in. thick or even more can be successfully spot-welded together. In some exceptional cases, spot welding is combined with brazing. The laminations are aligned by means of an adequate fixture and spot welded or stack welded. Prior to assembly, captive slugs are put in holes in the middle laminations. After spot welding the stack at a few points, the part is brazed in a "salt pot."

Where higher strength requirements and/or bigger workpieces are needed, arc welding is often employed as a fastening means, usually in combination with some suitable aligning means, but sometimes alone. In some exceptional instances, the weld beads, which are perpendicular to the stamping edges, are protruding externally. However, the more usual design consists of providing proper pockets by notching the blank contour. In this way the welds may be ground or sanded flush with the workpiece sides (see Fig. 3–62).

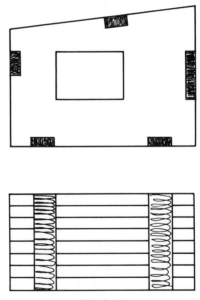

Fig. 3–62.

Very successful plug welded designs are produced (see Fig. 3–63). This technique allows differently shaped stampings to be perpendicularly joined to each other, and also to fasten layers of stacks together.

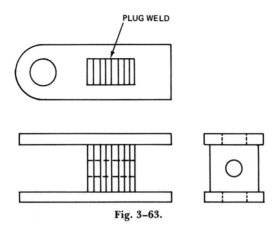

Fig. 3–63.

Protrusions are sometimes used for assembly of stacked stampings. By correct tool design, it is possible to obtain the right amount of interference fit between the male protrusions and the female depressions to enable the resulting press fit to perform light duty fastening in addition to the basic function of alignment. For heavier duty and increased safety, press fits may be supplemented with another assembly method such as brazing or welding.

There are quite a few instances where no standard assembly methods or means can be employed, so it is necessary to devise special assembly methods. Stamped rivets made from sheet metal have been successfully used for this purpose (see Fig. 3–64). A more complicated, but more efficient design employs

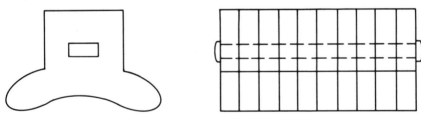

Fig. 3–64.

a specially shaped stamping which is then properly formed so that it aligns and simultaneously fastens the stack together (see Fig. 3–65).

In case of low accuracy requirements, no separate means are used for the assembly. Some boss, tab, or other blank portion which folds into matching notches, recesses, or slots in the mating parts is used (see Fig. 3–66).

Finally, the last method of joining the layers of stacked stampings, is with cements or epoxy resins adhesives (2). Practical data and reports on the subject are scarce, but they are very promising. Especially interesting in this respect are the different metal sheets available with plastic coatings which would facilitate the cementing process.

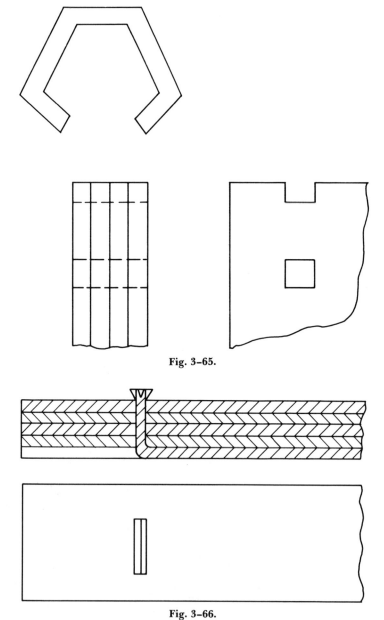

Fig. 3-65.

Fig. 3-66.

REFERENCES

1. *Alcoa Structural Handbook* (Philadelphia, Pa.: Aluminum Company of America, 1956), p. 262.
2. E. J. Bruno, ed., *Adhesives in Modern Manufacturing* (Dearborn, Mich.: Society of Manufacturing Engineers, 1970).

assembly methods

WELDED ASSEMBLIES

Basic Design of Brazed Joints

Brazed joints may be classified according to the shape of the components to be joined. Where metal stampings are involved, the following combinations are possible:

1) Flat sheets to flat sheets in the same plane
2) Flat sheets to flat sheets in a perpendicular or angular plane.

Flat parts in the same plane have two basic brazing joint designs, the butt joint and the lap joint. Any other kind of joint is a modification or a compromise between these two basic designs.

Butt joints are employed only when the appearance of the assembly is the main governing factor and when the joint thickness cannot be increased beyond the component thickness. The chief drawbacks of butt joints are: low strength because of unpredictable fillet formation, inadequate leak tightness, low electrical conductivity, and difficult preparation (machining) of the butting surfaces.

Since brazed joints should be so arranged that there be rather large adjoining surfaces which are united after the brazing process, butt joints should be avoided whenever possible. Instead, the following designs presented in increasing order of efficiency should be adopted.

1) Small flanges at the end of the components increase the contacting area (see Fig. 4–1)

Fig. 4–1.

2) The scarf joint is a compromise between butt joint and lap joint. The inclination angle varies between 15 and 45 deg according to stock thickness; it is inverse to stock gage (see Fig. 4–2)

73

Fig. 4-2.

3) In case of plates or thick sheets (over $\frac{1}{4}$ in.), the stepped joint provides a large contacting area (see Fig. 4-3)

4) Where two components of different thicknesses are concerned, the butt-lap joint gives very satisfactory results (see Fig. 4-4)

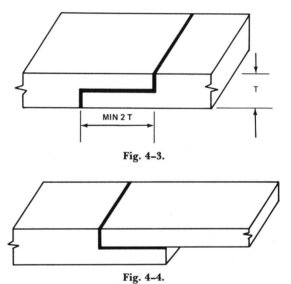

Fig. 4-3.

Fig. 4-4.

5) The best results, however, are obtained with lap or shear joints; they may be either straight (see Fig. 4-5) or joggled, and they insure larger joint surfaces

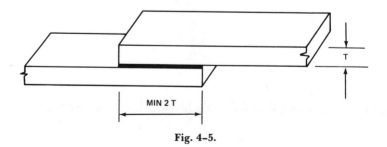

Fig. 4-5.

6) A strap joint is a variant of the joggled lap joint. This design employs additional sheet strips over the butt joint (see Fig. 4–6).

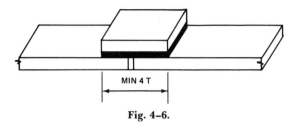

Fig. 4–6.

The second possible design combination is used to join flat parts with flat parts in an angular or perpendicular plane. In this design a simple butt joint is impossible. The possible methods of improving the strength of such joints are listed below:

1) Make a wedge entry for the filler by slightly bending the component end (see Fig. 4–7)
2) Transform the butt joint into a lap joint by providing a flange on one part (see Fig. 4–8)
3) Square or L shaped sections joined at 45 deg have natural wedge entry for the filler (see Fig. 4–9).

Where the joint is to be a corner one instead of a butt joint, make a flanged joint as shown in Figs. 4–10 and 4–11, or better yet make a crimped or seamed joint as shown in Fig. 4–12.

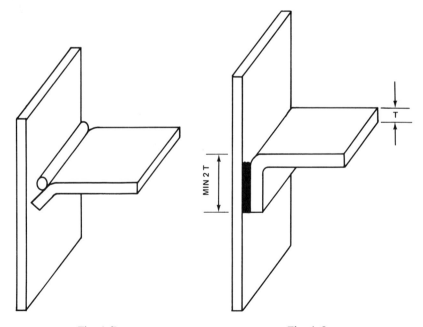

Fig. 4–7.   **Fig. 4–8.**

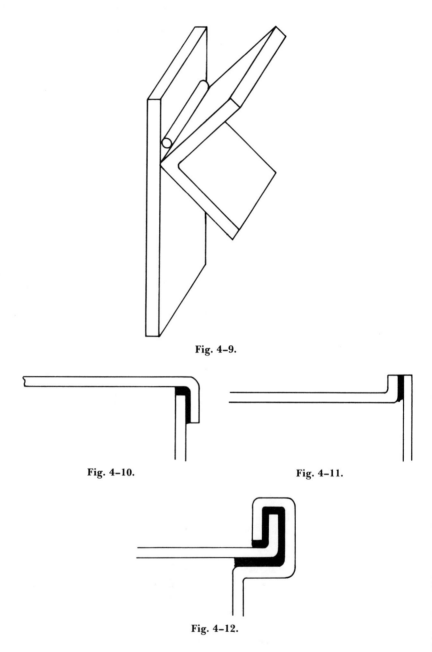

Fig. 4–9.

Fig. 4–10.   Fig. 4–11.

Fig. 4–12.

Always take into consideration the burr side of the components. The burr should not interfere with intimate contact of the parts. Therefore, the burr should never lay at the inside of the joints; it must be directed toward the outside as shown in Fig. 4–13. Also, the direction of the load should be taken into consideration. The joint itself should not be subjected to direct stresses (Fig.

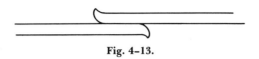

Fig. 4-13.

4-14 is wrong; Fig. 4-15 is right). If the rule must be broken, then the joint must be stressed for shear rather than for tension (Fig. 4-16 is wrong; Fig. 4-17 is right).

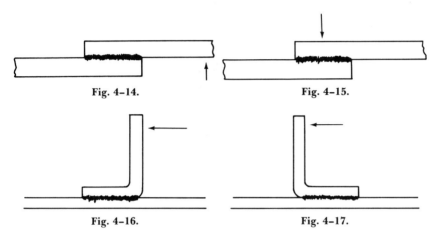

Fig. 4-14.   Fig. 4-15.

Fig. 4-16.   Fig. 4-17.

Design of Projection Welded Joints

The shape, form, size, and location of projections varies according to the nature and form of the parts, stock thickness, design of the joint, manufacturing processes of the parts, etc. The best shape is, of course, the round, both from the functional standpoint and the manufacturing standpoint, because it is less expensive, both in initial cost and in maintenance. However, in special instances, the projections may be made oval, oblong, or even rectangular. See the corresponding recommendations of the American Welding Society and the American National Standards Institute (ANS Y 14.10 1959/Sec. 10) for the size that the projection should be.

As to the location of the projections, there seems to be no general agreement; opinions and experiences are rather divergent. The following data, however, should be considered when locating the projection:

1) Make projections only in one of the two parts; only seldom are projections made in both parts
2) The projections must have rather high mechanical strength. Thus, if two parts are of different hardnesses, put the projections in the harder sheet. If two parts are of the same hardness, but of different thicknesses; put the projections in the heavier sheet. In case of materials of dissimilar electrical characteristics, locate the projections in the part of higher conductivity.
3) An exception to the above item might be where both parts are above .100 in. thick. Then the projections are best made in the thinner sheet.

4) In case of multiple weldings (more than two welding projections in a given part), the height of all projections should be the same, within ±.003. Projection welds are most widely employed for lap joints of two parallel sheet metal parts. Different methods are employed for the creation of the projections according to the stock thickness. In case of thin sheet (up to .080 in.) simple embossed dimples (buttons) are designed (see Figs. 4–18 and 4–19). Projections should not be located too near the stamping edge, nor too near each other. Leave about 3 to 5 times the stock thickness between projection centers and stamping edge; 5 to 10 times the stock thickness between adjacent projection centers. Take the lower values for heavy stock, and the higher values for light gage stock.

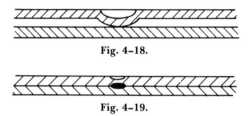

Fig. 4–18.

Fig. 4–19.

In medium gage stock (.25 to .50 in.), dome projections are created by protrusion (see Figs. 4–20 and 4–21). The dome type with relief (see Fig. 4–22) is an improvement. The latter is created to be filled with the melting metal. Without relief the squeezed metal of the projection may separate the two sheet metal parts.

In case of two sheets of different thicknesses, as mentioned above in item (2), the projections should be created in the thicker material. However, the shape and size of the projections are governed by the gage of the thinner part.

For very heavy stock (plates), or medium and heavy gage sheets where the welds must be invisible, the projections are swaged (staked) according to Fig. 4–23.

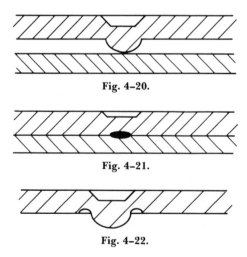

Fig. 4–20.

Fig. 4–21.

Fig. 4–22.

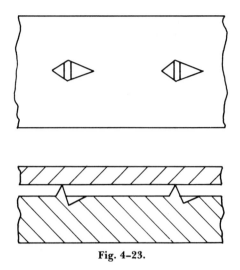

Fig. 4-23.

As mentioned above, the shape of embossed or extruded projections is usually round, but they may also be elongated, oblong, cross-shaped, ring-like, etc. Usually, only two sheet metal parts are welded together. However, in some cases three pieces are projection welded. In these instances, the projections are normally embossed in the outer components, although in some exceptional cases, the middle component has alternately spaced projections.

When two flat parts are welded together so that they form an angle (usually a right angle), the projections are normally on the surface against which the edge of the counterpart butts (see Fig. 4–24). Such design permits the easy creation of the projections. However, in some special cases, the main part is left flat and the projections are formed by trimming, notching, milling, or some

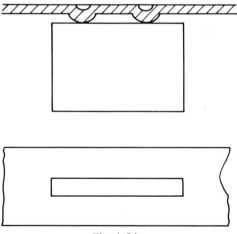

Fig. 4-24.

other way on the edge of the counterpart. Obviously, the main part is not always a flat sheet metal part; it may also be a tubing or a rod.

For components made of nonweldable material, or heat treated parts which cannot be subjected to welding, indirect projection welding may be used. Fig. 4–25 illustrates a practical example of clamping a flat spring between two coverplates.

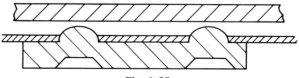

Fig. 4–25.

Fig. 4–26 represents an example where a punched stamping, which does not participate in the welding process, is firmly clamped or "sandwiched" between two outer parts. However, this design is not projection welding proper, because the projections are not flattened after welding. The process is a cross between projection welding and plain spot welding. Sometimes a small distance is left between the two covers which is then eliminated by the electrode-pressure. Such an arrangement increases the clamping pressure (see Fig. 4–27).

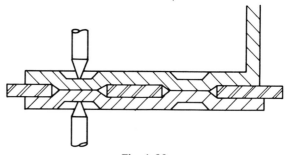

Fig. 4–26.

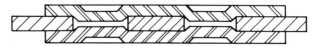

Fig. 4–27.

Design of Arc-Welded Joints

The first, basic recommendation consists of correctly shaping the matching ends of the components to be butt-welded together. The usual practice of two 45 deg wedges wastes welding rod and labor, and it does not provide the strongest joint (see Fig. 4–28). The 60 deg wedge shown in Fig. 4–29 is much better; but better yet is the double 60 deg wedge shown in Fig. 4–30.

During the welding process, great thermal expansions and contractions take

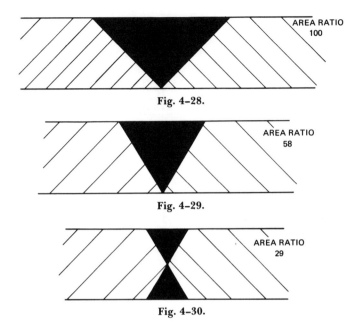

Fig. 4–28.

Fig. 4–29.

Fig. 4–30.

place. These are rather localized so that unless proper precautions are taken severe internal stresses are set up. In order to avoid them whenever possible, make the joint somewhat elastic. The solution illustrated in Fig. 4–31 is better than Fig. 4–32; Fig. 4–33 is better than Fig. 4–34.

In case of perpendicular joints of a thick part with a thin sheet, split the thick component or mill a groove in it, so that there are actually two thinner

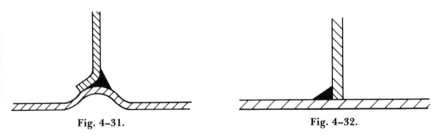

Fig. 4–31.   Fig. 4–32.

sections instead of one thick section (see Figs. 4–35 and 4–36). Also in this case a proper indentation or low rib in the thin sheet component avoids trouble caused by thermal contraction (see Fig. 4–37).

A comparatively weak joint (see Fig. 4–38) may be enormously strengthened with supplementary plates strategically located and welded as shown in Fig. 4–39. Observe the relieved corners; they give the advantage of easier welding without sacrificing strength. In addition, no justification exists for the structurally weak internal corner welds of the closed cabinet shown in Fig. 4–40. Only the external welds as illustrated in Fig. 4–41 are acceptable.

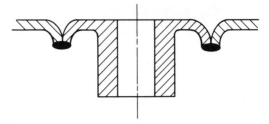

Fig. 4–33.

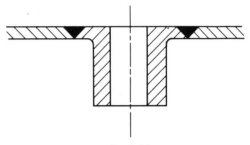

Fig. 4–34.

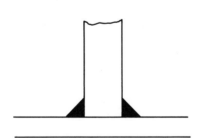

Fig. 4–35.

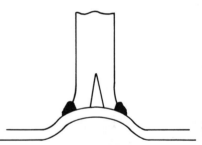

Fig. 4–36.

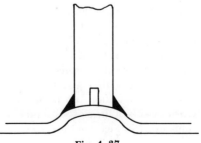

Fig. 4–37.

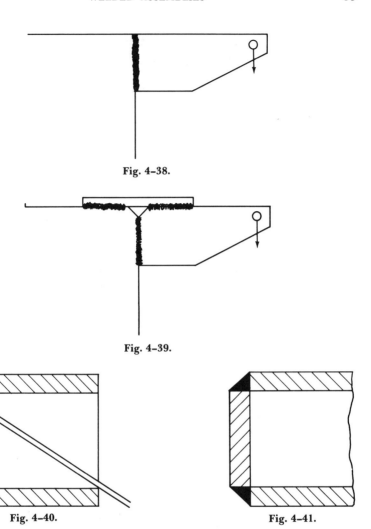

Fig. 4-38.

Fig. 4-39.

Fig. 4-40.   Fig. 4-41.

The first welds of cross reinforcing ribs are easily made as illustrated in
Fig. 4–42, but the second ones become internal joints with all the corresponding
drawbacks. The best practice is to let the rib protrude (see Fig. 4–43), or make
the rib flush to the surfaces as shown in Fig. 4–44, – always make the second row
of joints with easily accessible external welds.

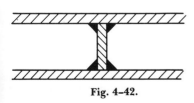

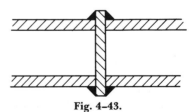

Fig. 4-42.   Fig. 4-43.

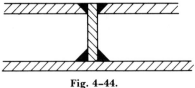

Fig. 4-44.

If a hollow, closed component must be welded to another or to a panel, vent holes must be provided in the hollow part so that the gases produced during the welding may easily escape (see Figs. 4-45 and 4-46).

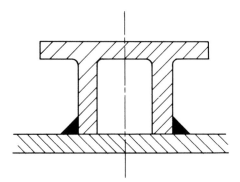

Fig. 4-45.

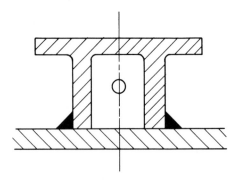

Fig. 4-46.

MECHANICAL ASSEMBLY METHODS

Basic Design of Seams

Seaming is widely used to join the sides of a tubular workpiece and/or the body of a can-like container with its top or bottom. This operation consists of permanently locking together two separate sheet metal parts or the two extremities of a given curved or bent thin component. This is done by forming the sides of the ~etal parts, joining them together, and mechanically locking the joint. While the chief goal of seams is assembly, they also reinforce the assembly. In addition, seams eliminate sharp edges that may cause injuries.

In a sense, curling and crimping are facets of seaming. However, in this chapter seaming designs are presented only in the strictest sense as folded (or curved) and flattened joints of sheet metal components. Seams of various designs are extensively employed for containers, drums, barrels, utensil bodies, sheet metal ducts, pipes for heating, ventilation and air conditioning, roofing sections, etc.

Seams are used where other kinds of mechanical assembly methods would be impractical or uneconomical and/or where welding would cause too much deformation and distortion. Besides, seaming often provides greater strength and resistance against high temperatures. Seams are normally used with comparatively thin metal sheets from .011 to .050 in. Heavier gage sheets require too much force for the seaming operation.

Seams may be classified according to the shape of the workpieces to be joined, and to the location of the seams with respect to the end of the components, as follows:

1) Straight seams for the body of tubular workpieces or simple formed stampings—jacket seams or longitudinal seams
2) Closed seams for joining the top or bottom to the tubular body of a can —circumferential seams
3) Closed seams for joining two tubular sections circumferentially; this is a variety of item (2), the difference being that the bottom is not a flat workpiece but a drawn shell or a piece of tubing.

The seam may be made directly, or in special cases, with the aid of an intermediary strap.

The most common seam for light gage sheets is the *simple or single* (grooved) *lock seam* also known as a standard seam or folded pipe seam. First, the ends are bent to acute angles, then they are interlocked, and the seam is closed (see Fig. 4–47). In the majority of cases, the two sections, the start and end of the tubular part, must be flush (see Fig. 4–48). The seam may be located outside (see Fig. 4–49) or inside (see Fig. 4–50) of the workpiece.

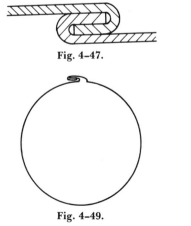

Fig. 4–47.   Fig. 4–48.

Fig. 4–49.   Fig. 4–50.

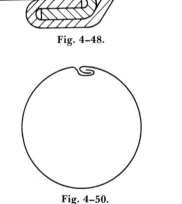

The single lock seam may be used not only on round workpieces but also on any form of sheet metal container: oval, square, rectangular, polygonal, etc. In case of angular cross sections, the seam may be located at any place on the periphery.

Where rather high strength conditions are necessary, a *double lock seam* is used. This is made in the following steps: the two parts are square bent with one leg longer than the other. The longer leg is bent over the shorter one (see Fig. 4–51). A standing seam is then formed (see Fig. 4–52). In some instances, this is the end product. Sometimes the seam is bent down and flattened against the workpiece body (see Fig. 4–53). Of course, a double lock seam may be internally or externally designed for any cross-sectional shape just like a single lock seam.

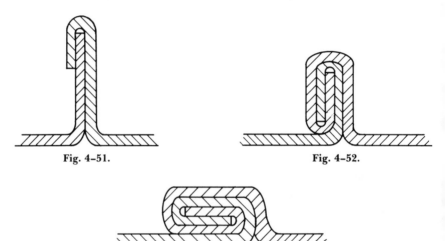

Fig. 4–51.   Fig. 4–52.

Fig. 4–53.

Up to this point all the seam designs are the *direct* type, i.e., the seams are formed on the workpiece ends. In *indirect* seaming, auxiliary pieces such as connector straps, cover joints, cover strips, and overlapping plates hold together the parts. These connecting elements are employed preferably on square or polygonal tubular parts (see Fig. 4–54). The width of a seam cannot be chosen

Fig. 4–54.

arbitrarily. Seams that are too small have no strength, are not sufficiently tight, and are difficult to assemble. Seams that are too large demand too much plastic flow, and the sheet metal is liable to crack or break. In addition, an unnecessary increase in stock usage results.

The correct seam size depends on the size of the component, stock thickness, shape, whether it is a bottom or jacket seam, whether the seaming method is manual or mechanical, etc. The seam for sheet metal up to $\frac{1}{32}$ in. thickness should be between $\frac{3}{16}$ and $\frac{1}{2}$ in. and proportionally wider for heavier material (see Figs. 4–55 through 4–57).

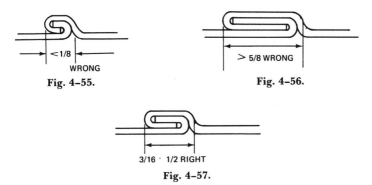

Fig. 4–55.   Fig. 4–56.

Fig. 4–57.

Design of Crimped Joints

Among the various assembly methods currently utilized for joining sheet metal components with other workpieces, crimping is one of the lesser used ones, even though the crimping method has excellent working characteristics. This versatile assembly method will aid many designs.

Crimping consists essentially of deforming one or both of the thin-walled workpieces in such a way that a firm, permanent joint is created. Note that the examples shown here may be considered seaming, but they are mostly border-line cases. Seaming is actually a kind of crimping.

Crimping unions may be roughly classified into the following various group-ings:

1) Matching beads (formed inward or outward)
2) Matching dimples (formed inward or outward)
3) Formed ribs or flanged unions
4) Holding beads
5) Special shapes.

Matching beads are used for crimping where pipes or tubings are involved. For joining two pieces of tubing, the following combinations may be used.

The O.D. of one matches the I.D. of the other. Fig. 3–49 illustrates the in-ward bead joint. In light cases of thin tubings made from soft, ductile metals, the two beads are formed together. To avoid much stress on heavier gages and/or harder metals, it is customary to first form the inner bead; then after assembly, form the outer bead against the inner one. If two tubings have the same dimensions, there may be the following arrangements: one of them is expanded for a short stretch and then assembled (see Fig. 3–49). Conversely, one of the tubing-ends may be contracted (reduced or necked) for a suitable length so that it may be introduced into the other tubing. Then the matching bead is formed, as explained above.

Tubing is joined to a full round bar by turning a groove in the bar and forming a matching bead in the tube against the groove. Cartridge shells are joined to slugs in a similar manner to the above, by pinching the shell end into a groove on the slug (see Fig. 4–58).

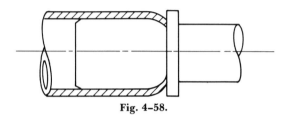

Fig. 4–58.

Matching dimples serve well when the requirements for the joints are not too severe and tightness is not essential. The holding strength of dimples is low, sometimes comparable to detachable assemblies. Instead of using beads or ribs, simple dimples or indentations are formed in both workpieces.

The simplest shape of dimples is the round, circular type (see Fig. 4–59). Sometimes, the indentations are rather deep and may assume the form of double slit bridges. On the other hand, only a single dimple is required (see Fig. 4–60) for very simple cases.

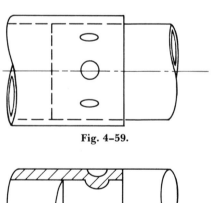

Fig. 4–59.

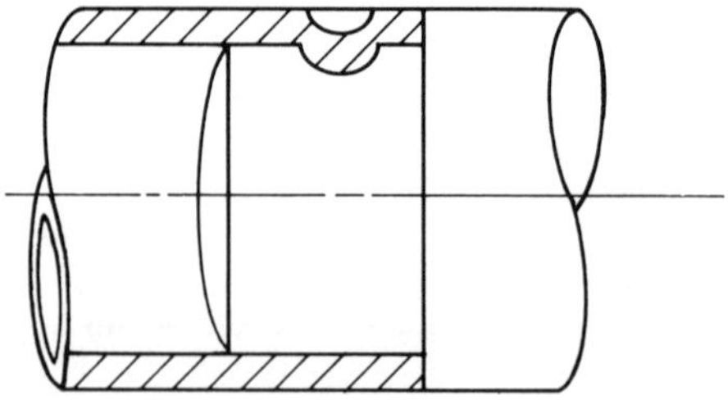

Fig. 4–60.

In the majority of applications (both components made from thin and comparatively soft metal), the dimples are made simultaneously in both pieces after assembly. But if the internal component is made from hard metal, it must be spot-drilled or grooved prior to assembly (see Fig. 4-60). On the other hand, if the internal workpiece is made from a rather soft material such as soft metal, wood, or rubber, the dimples are formed without any previous preparation of the inner workpiece.

Dimple-crimping is used not only on round workpieces, but also on flat and prismatic components. The assembly of a sheet metal stamping to a machined workpiece is very simple. The stamping, in which a properly located round hole has been previously punched, is introduced into a milled slot in the matching machined workpiece. Then with a simple, stub-nosed punch the machined workpiece is slightly deformed so that part of it enters the punched hole in the sheet metal stamping as shown in Figs. 4-61 and 4-62.

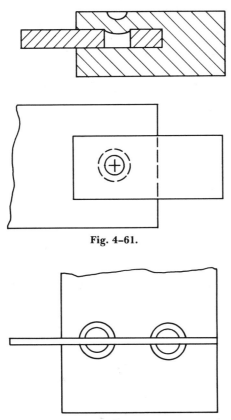

Fig. 4-61.

Fig. 4-62.

Parts to be crimped together usually have cylindrical shapes. However, quite often they have other cross-sectional shapes. In these instances, it is necessary to provide generous corner radii to facilitate the assembly.

Paper fasteners are a typical example of crimping design for holding together punched papers (see Fig. 4–63). The clips are assembled by crimping together a formed stamping (see Fig. 4–64) and a drawn cap (see Fig. 4–65).

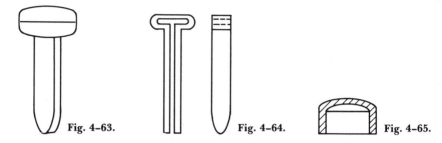

Fig. 4–63.   Fig. 4–64.   Fig. 4–65.

Crimping assembly cannot be employed indiscriminately; it has its limitations. The sheet metal of the components which are to be deformed should be thin, preferably under .030 in. The stock also must be quite soft either naturally or made so by a proper annealing process, or ductile with a comparatively low yield point. Copper, tin, brass, aluminum, and low-carbon steel have these material characteristics and are used extensively for crimping.

The crimping process may be effected either with mechanical means such as chisels, hand-punches in standard or special shapes or with press tools, bending machines, spinning, etc. Crimping may also be done with rubber rings or deformable plastic rings with or without the aid of press tools.

Assembly by Folding

One of the economical and popular indirect methods for joining light gage sheet metal parts is folding or bending over, wrapping, clinching, and strapping. A tab formed in one of the stampings is introduced into a matching slot or hole in the counterpart, and the tab then is folded over (see Fig. 4–66). According to the best bending techniques, a sheet metal stamping should always be bent so that the cutting burr is located to the inside of the bend. The finish-bend of the tab should always be in the same direction as the preliminary bend.

The best shapes for tab ends are the rounded (see Fig. 4–67), the half-round, the tapered (see Fig. 4–68), the triangular, or the square with chamfered corners

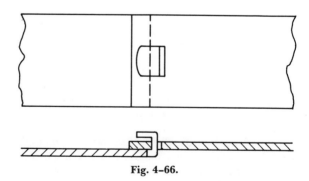

Fig. 4–66.

(see Fig. 4–69). These shapes are easier to introduce into the slots than the square contoured lug (see Fig. 4–70). This latter design should never be used for folding assemblies.

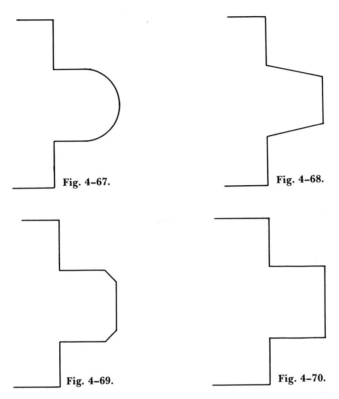

Fig. 4–67.   Fig. 4–68.

Fig. 4–69.   Fig. 4–70.

The matching slots should be made with dimensions that are somewhat larger than the tab thickness. The punches for slots, however, are very weak. Therefore, the shape of the slots should be changed whenever possible to reinforce the punches. Fig. 4–71 illustrates a very satisfactory solution of triangular slots. To reduce tool costs and tool maintenance, the possibility of using simple round holes instead of longitudinal slots should be examined. If the slots are simple notches, then there is no problem of punch strength.

One tab alone has little strength. In case of thin metal with sufficiently large stampings, it is better to use two or more lugs whenever possible. To get a multi-directional strength of the joint, the lugs should be alternately bent unless the stamping is U-shaped (see Fig. 4–71).

It is possible, of course, to join the two ends of a flat sheet metal blank, thus forming a piece of tubing (see Fig. 4–72), or a square or polygonal frame. Best strength conditions are achieved when the tabs are stressed for shear instead of bending as is usually the case. Fig. 4–73 illustrates this more favorable design. If space is insufficient for multiple-tabs, the lug can be longitudinally split, and the two halves of the lug bent in opposite directions for additional joint strength.

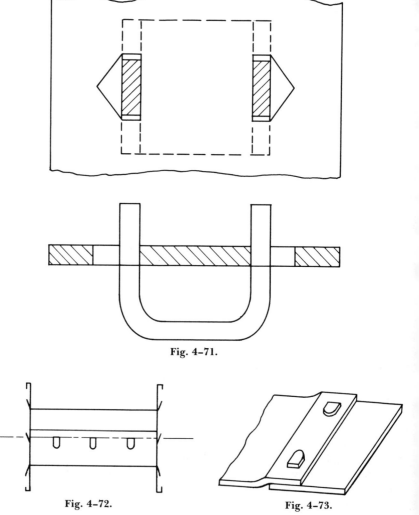

Fig. 4–71.

Fig. 4–72.

Fig. 4–73.

Sometimes the tabs must be located in the middle of the stampings. Such tabs (lanced tabs) are made by shear-forming.

In designing folding unions, be they end-joints or internal joints, i.e., with shear-formed tabs, the designer should always remember the basic rule of bending: the tabs must be bent across the lamination grain direction of the metal sheet at least 45 deg to prevent cracking and tearing of the stock.

Union by folding may be made without the previous formation of special tabs, or without the accompanying punching of slots. Simply bending the edges of a strip or of a stamping over other workpieces will often create a firm joint (see Fig. 4–74). Fig. 4–75 illustrates a simple folding without processing the counterpart.

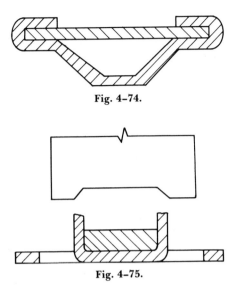

Fig. 4-74.

Fig. 4-75.

In some rare situations additional, auxiliary workpieces are designed for indirect union by folding. Fig. 4-76 illustrates a single stamping with the indirect folding of two ends of a strap.

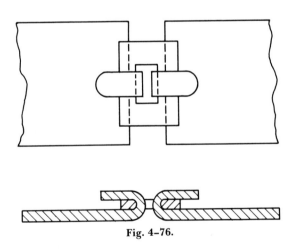

Fig. 4-76.

Assembly by folding probably started in the manufacturing of toys, but it has been adopted by many other industrial branches. It is very convenient for thin stampings, especially if they are lithographed, plated, or painted sheets where the surface finish would be impaired by soldering, brazing, welding, etc. Other intrinsic advantages of the folding method have already been mentioned. Complete spools are made from sheet metal (see Fig. 4-72) by fold-joining a rectangular stamping provided with tabs and two round discs.

Stress Relieving of Bonded Joints

Components have always been bonded or cemented on a large scale; however, it has been restricted chiefly to nonmetallic objects. Lately, however, the development of suitable bonding materials has extended bonding for permanent joining to metallic parts. Since bonded joints have comparatively low strength, it is good practice to design them so that some additional mechanical method relieves the load or stress that may be applied to the joint. The same methods may be successfully employed for soldered joints and for brazed assemblies.

To bond sheet metal components, lap joints are used almost exclusively. The strength of the union, other factors being equal, is proportional to the contacting areas of the joint. This area, however, cannot be increased indiscriminately. This is the reason for providing aids in the form of aligning and stress-relieving details. A simple method consists of providing tabs, flaps, or bent legs which lean against the outer contour of the counterpart or work in combination with punched holes, slots, or notches made in the counterpart (see Fig. 4–77).

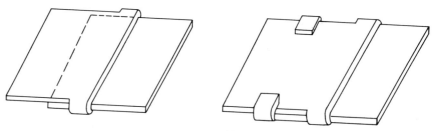

Fig. 4–77.

Sometimes mechanical fasteners are used. The most popular fastening device is a hollow rivet, but sometimes a full rivet, screw, and/or spot welding is used. Whenever greater strength and rigidity are required, seams are used. According to the direction and kind of loads and stresses and their magnitude, a suitable design is chosen from among the infinite variety of possible seam designs.

A simple design that enormously increases the strength of a joint, if the resistance of the joint is not entirely dependent upon bonding, is illustrated in Fig. 4–78. Simple brackets are similar in that they should not be bonded only (see Fig. 4–79), but arranged so that the load will be resisted mechanically (see 4–80); a small flange is a great help in this case (see Fig. 4–81).

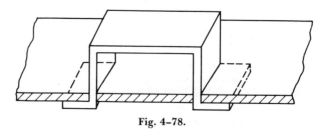

Fig. 4–78.

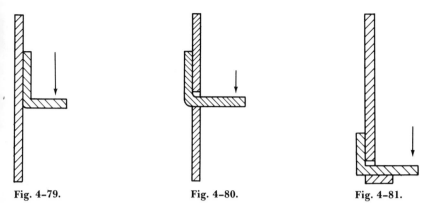

Fig. 4–79.   Fig. 4–80.   Fig. 4–81.

Joints where the load is applied perpendicular to the joint-plane must be avoided since it is loaded in tension (see Fig. 4–82). Joints should be designed so that the load will be applied in the same plane of the joint thereby loading it in shear. This means that butt joints must be transformed into lap joints. This can be achieved either by means of supplementary squares (see Fig. 4–83), or by suitably forming a rib in the panel or counterpart (see Fig. 4–84).

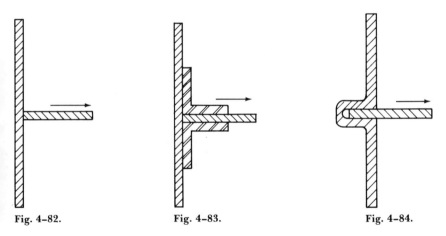

Fig. 4–82.   Fig. 4–83.   Fig. 4–84.

Stacking is helpful. The shelves of a filing cabinet are made with matching slots, and thus, they hold each other properly in place. The ends of the shelves (and of the vertical separators) are then bonded to the cabinet walls. No simple butt joint can be used to fix a piece of tubing or a full rod into a panel or through a sheet metal component. An embossed hole increases the contacting surfaces and changes the butt joint into a lap joint. If embossing of the through hole is not practical, then a separate flange must be provided. If the end of the tubing must be joined with the flat part, then the end may be flared out (see Fig. 4–85). Standard flanges may be located either at the end (see Fig. 4–86), or at any intermediate position. Polygonal rods or tubings are bonded best to shear-formed tabs created in the counterparts.

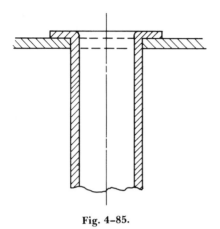

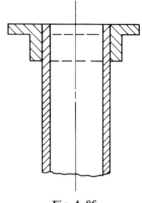

Fig. 4–85.   Fig. 4–86.

Bayonet Locks

Bayonet locks are temporary joints for assembling two components which must be easily and quickly joined or separated. The joining is effected so that the telescoping components are first united axially and then turned or slid radially. One of the components carries protuberances which are guided in matching slots, canals, or grooves in the counterpart. For disassembling, the two movements are reversed. In the great majority of cases the components have cylindrical, mostly tubular, shapes though sometimes flat parts may be joined with bayonet locks.

Classification of bayonet lock designs takes into account the safety or clamping pressure with which the joint is held together. Classification is as follows:

1) Wedge action
2) Bolting
3) Spring action.

The most common application of bayonet locks consists of joining a lid or cover with the corresponding cylindrical shaft or case (see Fig. 4–87). Usually

Fig. 4–87.

two diametrally located pins are designed on the shaft with matching slots in the lid: in large diameter parts, three or four or even more are inserted. Of course, the inclined portion of the slot must be sufficiently long so that a complete closure is achieved before the pin can reach the end of the slot. The inclination angle is small for high self-locking action; on the other hand if it is too small, it requires more radial travel. On lids made from sheet metal which has a certain elasticity, it may be small.

If the shaft is a hollow tube, pipe, closed bottom drawn container, or can, the pins are riveted in place. Sometimes the rivet receives a supplementary outer head for greater safety. For light duty, the riveted pin may be substituted by tabs created by double slitting and further bending (see Fig. 2–29). In the case of tubular counterparts, the location of the pins and slots may be inverted, i.e., the pins are then on the lid and the slots in the counterpart. The pin is not always a separate item. For light duty, it may be formed as a pressed nib stamped in the cover (see Fig 4–88).

The slots weaken the end of the tubing. Therefore, in the case of light gage walls, the punched slots should be replaced by embossed closed ribs (see Fig. 4–89).

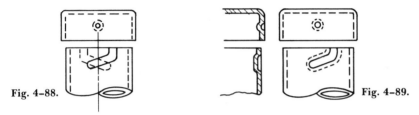

Fig. 4–88.   Fig. 4–89.

If the joint does not have to be absolutely tight, or if the clearance between the O.D. of the can and the I.D. of the cover is large, matching inclined ribs are formed by embossing. This design is essentially a double-pitched lead-threaded joint.

In jig and fixture building, bayonet locks are occasionally employed for quick-action clamping of workpieces. A similar device is a coupling nut for fixtures used for turning round workpieces. The clamping is effected by bayonet lock.

Interchangeable camera lenses use bayonet locks. The lens has three wings (interrupted flanges) whose upper surfaces are inclined. The camera is provided with a flanged ring in which three openings are notched out (see Fig. 4–90). The wings on the lens pass through the notched-out openings; then the lens is turned about 60 deg to clamp it in place.

A less expensive design for the preceding case consists of providing both parts with a fine pitch thread from which are milled away three portions each. The male part is simply introduced into the female part and then is turned less than 60 deg to provide a firm joint. Quick-acting couplings for pipes, hoses, etc. are made in this way (see Fig. 4–91).

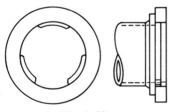

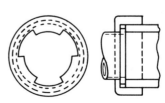

Fig. 4–90.   Fig. 4–91.

When parts will be exposed to vibrations while in service (for instance, lamps for automobiles), bolting is used to assemble the components. The slot is made in three portions: an axial one for introduction, a radial one for the union and at the end of the latter, a reverse axial slot where the pin is held. A proper compressive spring provides the necessary pressure for maintaining the joint firmly in a closed position (see Fig. 4–92). Lanced (or slit and bent) tabs may be used instead of pins in some applications.

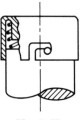

Fig. 4–92.

In those cases where it is not possible to employ compression springs for maintaining the joint under pressure, any other locking method may be employed; e.g., a spring actuated indexing pin which must be pulled out to disassemble the union. In other instances, the bolting is effected by means of screws which function also as aligning pins; a pipe flange may be fastened in the same way.

In many cases of light duty, pipes may be joined by taking advantage of the elasticity of tabs formed on the flanges of the pipe. On the counterpart-flange two corresponding notches are provided through which the pipes are assembled; a proper turn against a stop in the form of an embossed rib completes the joint. Rounding of the flange sections facilitates the assembly (see Fig. 4–93). The tabs may be formed by joggling if the two tubular parts have different diameters.

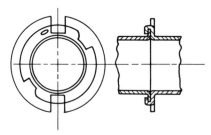

Fig. 4–93.

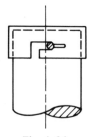

Fig. 4–94.

In exceptional cases, the design illustrated in Fig. 4–94 is employed. The pin is slightly larger in diameter than the slot width. During the assembly, the slit at the end of the slot permits the slot to open. This spring-action firmly grips the pin.

miscellaneous design items

ALIGNMENT OF STAMPINGS

In this section, the most widely used practical methods for correctly aligning and thus correctly assembling metal stamping components are discussed. The aligning methods currently employed may be classified according to various standpoints: permanence of joint, relative mobility, direct or indirect means, etc. However, the chief criterion is the requirement of accuracy. According to the allowed tolerances, the alignment may be of low, medium, or high accuracy. Every type and kind of aligning method belongs to one of these three groups.

Low Accuracy Alignment

The simplest, most direct method for aligning two flat or formed metal stampings consists of shear-forming two tabs in one of the stampings, and then introducing the two tabs into two corresponding round holes in the other component (see Fig. 5-1). Longitudinal slots may be used instead of holes to improve

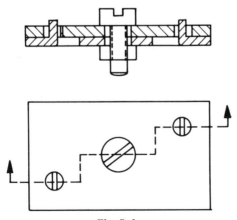

Fig. 5-1.

the accuracy. Of course, the precision depends on the allowed clearance between tab dimensions and slot dimensions. In the majority of cases, the lanced tabs also serve as fasteners, either by folding the tabs or twisting the end of the tab. The tabs may be bent or formed at the end or the side of the components

99

instead of lancing them in the middle of the stampings. Also the parallel slitting and stretching of the metal between the slits, also known as double louvering, is used in combination with round holes (see Fig. 5–2). In some cases, simple notches are substituted for slots (see Fig. 5–3), or the tabs may be bent around the sides of the counterpart without the benefit of notches.

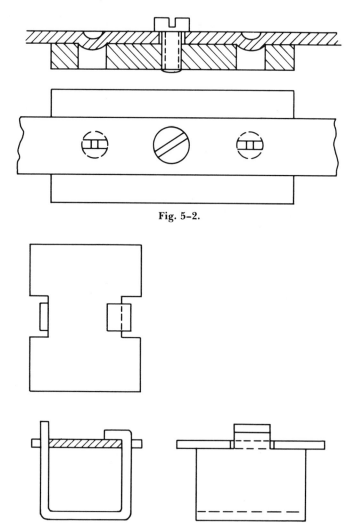

Fig. 5–2.

Fig. 5–3.

Medium Accuracy Alignment

Where the accuracy of the relative location of the parts is not very strict, the assembly devices also take over the task of alignment. This is often the case when joining metal stampings with screws or rivets, provided that in an assembly there are at least two such fasteners. The accuracy of the assembly is somewhat improved if flat-headed screws are used (see Fig. 5–4). These screws centralize the assembly better than through-bolts which need holes with additional clearance.

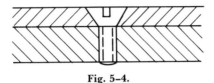

Fig. 5–4.

High Accuracy Alignment

For best conditions, two ordinary cylindrical or tapered dowel pins put in properly punched and shaved or reamed holes are recommended (see Fig. 5–5). The greater the distance between the two pins, the higher the accuracy of alignment.

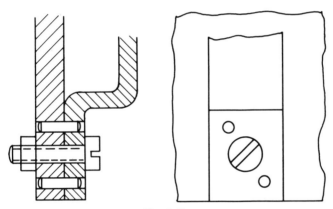

Fig. 5–5.

In case of comparatively heavy material, instead of separate dowel pins, protrusions may be formed in the stamping that are matched up with punched or drilled holes in the counterpart (see Fig. 5–6). On the other hand, if the stampings in question are made from rather light gage material, then the dowel may be

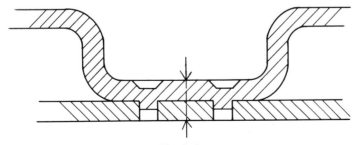

Fig. 5–6.

made in the form of an extruded boss (see Fig. 2–18). Both the protrusions and the extruded bosses may also be used for fastening purposes.

If there is no space for extra rivets or pins of any kind, then the alignment may be effected in either of the following ways:

1) Stripper bolts—screws with a threaded point for fastening and a smooth shank for alignment (see Fig. 5–7)

2) Precision bushings—the bushings are put in holes to align the parts; bolts are put through the bushings to fasten the parts (see Fig. 5–8).

Fig. 5–7.

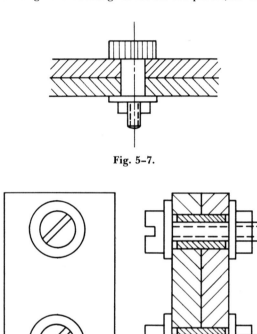

Fig. 5–8.

Dowels of any kind perform well in combination with holes, usually specially made for the dowels. However, if space for the aligning holes is not available, the locating must be done with the outer contour of the workpieces. For this purpose the counterpart and sometimes also the main stamping must be properly formed:

1) By adequate shaping of the components, a matching assembly insures satisfactory alignment between the parts

2) Ribs strategically located as straight or curved protuberances, perfectly align the stampings (see Fig. 5–9). This is a very popular method with molded plastic, ceramic, powdered metal, and die cast parts

3) If the counterpart is sufficiently thick, slots may be milled in it for aligning the stamping (see Fig. 5–10). The design of Fig. 5–11 requires a small

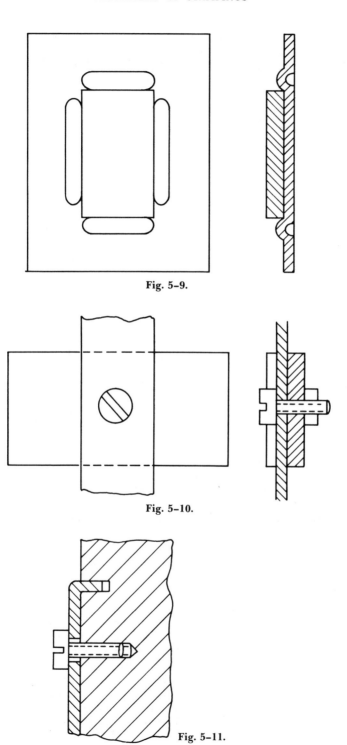

Fig. 5–9.

Fig. 5–10.

Fig. 5–11.

flange to be bent at the end of the stamping and a properly matching narrow slot in the counterpart

4) If the counterpart is machined, cast, extruded, or molded, a proper shoulder which butts against the stamping aligns the parts (see Fig. 5-12).

In some instances, combinations among the various methods of using dowels and processed counterparts may obtain the highest possible accuracy at comparatively low costs. The following general combinations are possible: ribs and dowels, ribs and notches (see Fig. 5-13), tabs and dowels, and tabs and ribs.

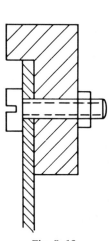

Fig. 5-12.

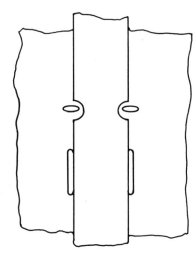

Fig. 5-13.

Spacing Metal Stampings in Assemblies

The designer is often faced with the task of assembling two or more components which must be separated by an exact gap. This is a problem in axial alignment in contrast to radial alignment dealt with up to this point in this chapter. Such assemblies may be immovable (the relative position of the two parts is permanently fixed), or movable (one of the parts may slide, rotate, pivot, etc. with respect to the other).

The first, obvious solution for this task consists of providing a separate spacer which is usually a simple shaped part. To avoid the additional cost of making and handling another component, one or both of the parts involved may receive bosses or projections to serve as spacers. Several design possibilities in sheet metal stampings will eliminate the problem of using separate spacers. The figures listed below illustrate the most frequently used spacing methods for sheet metal stampings. They are presented in a sequence of increasing size.

For small distances, *protrusions* are used. Bosses of *extruded holes* are excellent spacers (see Fig. 5-14). Sometimes they must be machined before assembly to get higher accuracy with closer tolerances. Pipeless tubings with round fins for refrigerator parts are made by brazing together small stampings with concentric extruded holes (see Fig. 5-15). By combining extruded hole patterns with plain punched holes, special filtering sheets are created which allow the filtered liquid

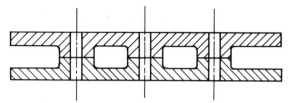

Fig. 5–14.

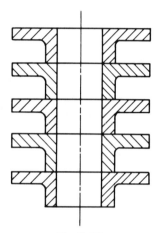

Fig. 5–15.

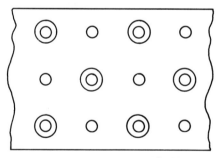
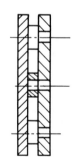

Fig. 5–16.

to get through between the filtering sheet and the solid backing plate (see Fig. 5–16).

Embossed dimples formed in the middle of metal sheets are used sometimes as spacers (see Fig. 3–52). Other design detail possibilities are reinforcing *ribs* which are created either by embossing or by compound bending. Fig. 5–17 illustrates a simple case of a circular bead at the bottom of a shell separating the stamping from the table upon which it is located. Properly formed bent and/or shear-formed *tabs* and *legs* that are off-set or Z-formed, etc. allow comparatively large distances to be held.

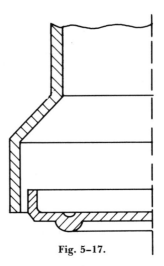

Fig. 5-17.

RELIEVING SCREWS FROM BENDING STRESSES

If clamping bolts are insufficiently tightened, or if they loosen during work because of vibration, thermal expansions and contractions, sudden changes in loads, etc., they may be subjected to undue bending and shear stresses under certain circumstances. Several practical methods have been devised for relieving the fastening bolts from the stresses.

One stress-relieving method is to use cylindrical or tapered dowel pins designed to secure comparatively small transversal loads, and chiefly for semi-permanent unions (see Fig. 5-18). The pins are normally located in holes

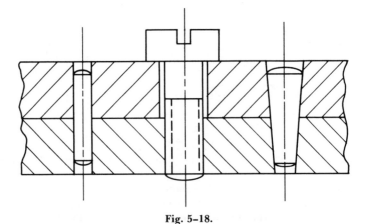

Fig. 5-18.

punched in the parts for that purpose. Cylindrical pins are usually driven permanently into one of the components (drive-in fit), and pushed into the corresponding hole in the counterpart for easy separation.

Cylindrical dowel pins are less expensive, but with them the assembly is not so easy to separate. Besides, they become easily galled or scored. Therefore, especially for long holes, the tapered design is preferred.

Sometimes the dowel pins are not separate items, but may be created by suitable forming of the workpieces. In case of die castings or plastic moldings, a cylindrical or tapered protuberance functions as a proper dowel pin. In case of components made from heavy gage sheet metal, protrusions (see Fig. 5–19) may be substituted for the dowel pin.

A stripper-bolt is essentially a precision screw with an enlarged body which must be pushed or driven into a hole which has been reamed simultaneously in the two or more workpieces (see Fig. 5–20). According to the kind of fit, this

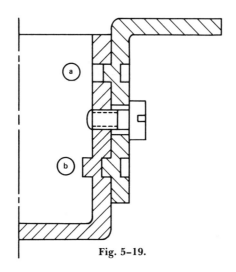

Fig. 5–19.

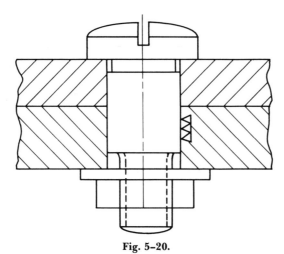

Fig. 5–20.

method allows comparatively large dynamic loads. Because of the close toler-ances, however, this method is rather expensive.

Alignment bushings offer a much less expensive solution. (see Fig. 5–21). These longitudinally split steel bushings with proper spring action are driven

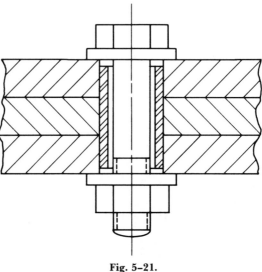

Fig. 5–21.

into drilled or punched holes without the need for expensive shaving or ream-ing. A standard bolt passes through the interior of the bushing. Thus, space is saved because there is no need for the dowel pins. The pre-load on the bushing resists the bending or shearing forces and avoids shifting of the workpieces. In cases of excessive transversal load stresses, the bushings must be made full (closed) and located in correctly bored holes with a push fit or drive fit.

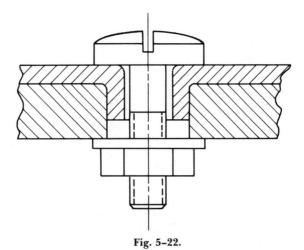

Fig. 5–22.

If one of the components is made from sheet metal, an extruded hole may be formed for the alignment bushing. The boss is then used for stress-relieving and aligning while the fastening screw passes through the hole (see Fig. 5–22). For light duty, lanced tabs may be employed for stress-relieving the fastening of the additional workpiece (see Fig. 2–31).

TOLERANCES IN METAL STAMPINGS

The approach to tolerance specifications for stamping should not be the same as the approach for machined parts. Machined parts allow closer tolerances than stampings. Correct dimensioning and determination of tolerances for stampings should be realistic and conform with the true functional requirements.

The best basic procedure consists in taking advantage of empirical, practical data taken from actual products which are functionally similar to the new product in question. If there is no previous experience to work with, then the following simple procedure should be taken as a guide for the determination of tolerances. Minimal clearance between operating components is the space that barely permits assembling of the components and their correct operation under service conditions. Maximum clearance is the distance that still allows proper functioning of the assembly. In this way, the two tolerance limits are established with a good approximation.

Practical Data

Some data on tolerances in metal stampings are presented here as a guide. These data have been collected in actual practice and reflect the usual commercial practice in the field. They are recommendations; deviations from them are quite frequent. They refer to short run jobs in which tools of the lowest cost are anticipated. Closer tolerances are possible in all cases; however, they would require more sophisticated tooling and manufacturing processes which, of course, increase production costs.

Flat Stampings

In every stamping, the die-cut surfaces are never completely straight or perpendicular to the general surface of the stamping. It is composed of a land which is smooth and parallel, and a break which is uneven, rough, and tapered (see Fig. 2–2). The land is usually smaller than the break in a hole or on a blank. In both cases always measure or check the land portion.

Tolerances for punched holes and outer contours for blanks vary with stock quality, thickness, and hardness, with the size and shape of the part, with the condition, design, and accuracy of the tool, with the number of stations in progressive dies, and other circumstances.

Fig. 5–23 presents the tolerances suggested by the Small Lot Stamping Institute. The values reported in Fig. 5–23 refer to light gage stock (up to .031 in.). In case of medium gage stock (up to .062 in.), tolerances must be increased by about 25 to 50 percent; for heavy gage stock (over .062 in.) tolerances increase by 100 to 200 percent.

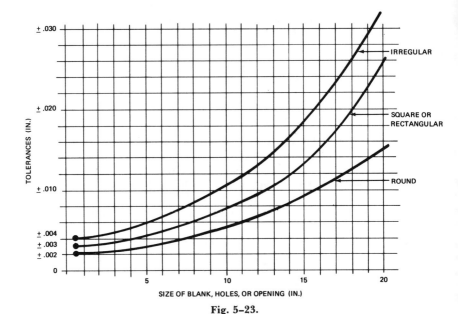

Fig. 5–23.

Tolerances for center distances between holes located in the same plane depend chiefly upon the corresponding production methods:

1) If punched simultaneously with the same die: ±.003
2) If punched with separate, single operation dies: ±.005
3) If punched in progressive dies, made in separate stations, according to quantity of stations between operations and type of progression gage: ±.005 to ±.015.

Tolerances for hole location from the edge of a stamping or from a bend are as follows:

1) Light and medium stock (up to .062 in.): ±.008 to ±.010
2) Heavy stock (.062 to .125 in.):   ±.015 to ±.020
3) Very heavy stock (over .125 in.):   ±.030 to ±.035.

Holes in bent legs must always be located from the inside. In this way the variations of sheet metal thickness do not influence the location tolerances.

If closer tolerances are required than is stated in the above paragraph, the holes must be punched after forming. This means lower production rates, higher tooling costs, and, therefore, higher prices per workpiece.

In case of incomplete blanks, the tolerances must be increased because of the inherent lower accuracy of production techniques:

Parting: Short lengths (up to 6 in.): ±.005 to ±.008
           Long stampings: ±.010 to ±.015

Cutting off: Light gage
                short lengths: ±.015
                long parts: ±.030
           Heavy gage:
                short length: ±.025
                long parts: ±.040

Width tolerances for both parting and cutting off correspond to commercial tolerances for slitting strips and coils. Concentricity is the relationship of one dimension to another. Tolerances on concentricity should be specified only if necessary for correct functioning. Commercial concentricity tolerances are: .010 to .020 in. TIR.

The chief governing factors for flatness are the material temper and the tool design. Under ordinary circumstances, a flatness of .005 to .010 in/in TIR can be maintained. If closer tolerances are required, some corrective operation such as coining or spanking, planishing, straightening, or grinding is needed. Such corrective operations increase costs. Designers should avoid the frequent mistake of confusing flatness with parallelism.

The designer should specify burr height limits only if the function of the parts demands it. Removal of burrs or removal of sharp edges should be avoided because of the additional expense.

Formed Stampings

The average dimensional tolerances in workpieces formed in *press-brakes* are:
1) For regular, small parts: ±.030
2) For large and complicated shapes: ±.060 or more

The average dimensional tolerances in workpieces formed in *dies* are:
1) Small workpieces, or portions of work: ±.010
2) Off-sets (see Fig. 5–24): ±.010
3) Channel forming (see Fig. 5–25): tolerances on dimensions A and B can be held within .010

Fig. 5–24.

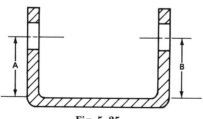

Fig. 5–25.

4) Always specify angle tolerances in degrees, not in straight dimensions — usual tolerance limits are ±1 deg, except when one leg is shorter than 1 in.; then the tolerances are ±2 deg
5) Always specify internal bending radii, never outer radii — tolerances on radii should be liberal: ±.010 for $R \leq .060$ and ±.020 for $R \geq .060$.

Drawn Shells

For drawn shells no standard, customary tolerance values exist. Every plant has its own standards. In establishing such tolerances for drawn shells, take into account the following points:
1) Wall thickness of drawn shells deviates from bottom thickness; some portions are thinner, some portions thicker
2) Do not specify both O.D. and I.D. with close tolerances — only one of them can be reasonably held.

Stock Thickness Tolerances

The standard thickness tolerances given by sheet metal manufacturers are from about 10 to 20 percent. These allowed thickness variations prohibit close tolerance limits on form and shapes. Fig. 5-26 illustrates how the thickness variations influence the accuracy of formed stamping shapes.

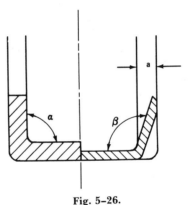

Fig. 5-26.

In channel forming (see Fig. 5-26), the clearance between the punch and the female die cavity (α) must be accurately estimated for the highest thickness value. Consequently, the bending angle will be different according to whether the stock is on the high or low limit of the commercial tolerance. The designer should keep these facts in mind before setting up tolerance limits for formed parts.

ALLIED OPERATIONS

Only in exceptional cases are metal stampings shipped in the condition "as stamped." Apart from the fact that they may be subjected to some special pressing operations such as coining, swaging, stamping, riveting, sizing, press forging, etc., usually some special finishing or other operation is performed on them. Only the most frequent secondary operations are discussed.

Heat Treatment

Annealing consists of heating a piece of metal and cooling it very slowly so that the hardness or stresses induced in the part by previous heat treatment or cold-working will be removed. Heating a piece of steel to a given temperature and then *quickly* cooling it increases the hardness of the part. Adding carbon to the surface of low-carbon iron-base alloys is another way of hardening parts.

Cyanidizing is still another means of hardening the surface of parts by using carbon, nitrogen absorption, and heat treatment. This treatment is usually performed on low-carbon steels. Nitriding or the addition of nitrogen to iron-base alloys also hardens these steels.

Machining

1) Deburring (mechanically) — removing the cutting burrs by means of some machining operation
2) Drilling — opening holes in workpieces with drills, i.e., with a chip-forming operation
3) Tapping — forming female threads in holes by means of a chip-removal operation
4) Reaming — converting the rough surfaces of drilled holes into smooth, concentric holes
5) Counterboring — machining cylindrical recesses for square-headed fasteners
6) Countersinking — machining a tapered recess for sunken head (flush) fasteners
7) Milling — machining the outer contour of stamping, with a multi-toothed cutter and rotating movement
8) Broaching — machining the outer and/or internal contour of stampings with a multi-toothed cutter, with a straight, line-movement
9) Grinding — chip removal with abrasive wheels
10) Beading — forming beads or circular ribs around the edge or in the middle of workpieces made from sheet metal.

Cleaning

1) Washing — removing dirt and foreign matter from the stampings by means of liquids
2) Degreasing — removing oil or grease from the surface of stampings by means of vapor or solvents
3) Steaming — removing dirt, oil, grease, and foreign matter from the surface of stampings, by means of vapor
4) Vapor blasting also known as liquid honing — polished metal by bombardment with an air-ejected liquid containing fine solid particles in suspension. If an impeller wheel is used to propel the suspension, the process is called wet blasting or hydroblasting.
5) Pickling — removing surface oxides from metals by means of adequate chemical or electrochemical action.

Surface Treatment

Tumbling is the most popular method for improving the appearance of metal objects and for removing small burrs. The workpieces are rotated in a polygonal barrel together with some abrasive media until the surface imperfections are removed. Tumbling may be performed dry or wet, the latter being the most often used method.

Buffing is a method that produces a smooth, brilliant surface by contacting the workpiece with a rotating fabric wheel coated with proper materials. Smoothing metal surfaces by means of the use of fine abrasive materials is usually referred to as polishing. Another method of cold working metal surfaces by metal shot jets is called shot peening.

Surface Coating

1) Anodizing—forming a conversion coating on a metal surface, usually aluminum, by anodic oxidation
2) Painting—application of paints of different colors
3) Phosphate coating—forming an adherent phosphate coating on a metal surface immersed in a suitable water phosphate solution
4) Rust preventive dipping—coating a metal surface with a suitable solution to prevent oxidation of the metal
5) Plating—coating surfaces with a metallic substance for decoration or for protection against corrosion or wear
6) Metallizing—forming a metallic coating by atomized spraying with molten metal or by vacuum deposition.

Assembly

Various components are joined to make subassemblies or to complete assemblies.

Inspection

Every batch of stampings must be inspected before shipping. Normally, a spot check is sufficient, but in some instances, especially where requirements are stringent, a hundred percent inspection is necessary.

STANDARDIZATION OF METAL STAMPING DESIGN

Only a few details can be standardized in metal stamping designs. These are:
1) Quality of material
2) Thickness of material
3) Strip width
4) Hole sizes.

Quality of Material

The designer can make substantial savings through wise selection of material. The specifications of the manufacturers for sheet metal lists a large number of types with the differences in characteristics and performance to be expected. Many times a compromise choice will enable one type to be used in several production runs. For instance, steel sheets, which are most often used, are classified according to manufacturing processes (cold or hot rolled), analysis, surface finish, temper, drawability, etc. Specific requirements which must be satisfied may demand special material for deep drawing, extrusion, electrical laminations, or stainless characteristics; however, practical experience shows that a few steel brands are sufficient for satisfactory performance for the majority of cases. The same is true also for alloy steels, nonferrous metals, and their alloys.

If only a few material types can fulfill the needs of a particular company, several advantages are realized:

1) Greater quantities of the same kind of material are purchased each time; this means lower prices because of higher quantity discounts
2) The overall quantity of material held in storage becomes smaller even if the quantity per brand or size is greater; since the number of types is drastically decreased, the total quantity of stock is lower
3) Consequently, the corresponding financial investments for material will remain reduced
4) The probability for supply troubles and mix-ups will be less; easier, clearer control of stock usually results in prompt replacement and timely procurement of new material.

Thickness of Material

It is very convenient to limit the material thicknesses to a few values and gages, and to choose from them one for any new component or product. In this way, as with stock quality standardization discussed in the previous paragraph, it is possible to take advantage of warehouse inventories and realize other advantages.

The following sheet thicknesses in inches are recommended for standardization:

.015,　.018,　.024,　.030,　.036,　.048,　.060,　.075,

$\frac{1}{32}$,　$\frac{1}{16}$,　$\frac{3}{32}$,　$\frac{1}{8}$,　$\frac{5}{32}$,　$\frac{1}{4}$,　$\frac{5}{16}$, and $\frac{3}{8}$.

Strip Width

It is good practice to standardize strip widths with $\frac{1}{16}$ in. increments for small sizes (up to about 1 in.), and with increments of $\frac{1}{8}$ in. for medium and larger sizes.

Holes

For round holes, the shape chosen in the majority of cases, the corresponding ANSI Standard (ANS Y 14.10-1959) recommends that the basic diameters should be governed by standard drill sizes whenever possible. Unfortunately, this seems rather difficult to do because the commercially available standard round punches do not follow this recommendation. The punches in question are either in increments of $\frac{1}{64}$ in. or of .010 in. In the first case with only one exception ($\frac{1}{4}$ in.), every standard drill size both numbers and letters are odd fractions. In the second case, round decimal fraction sizes, the situation is somewhat better; about half of the number sizes coincide, but even with these it is not possible to do as the ANSI Standard suggests. Therefore, it is recommended that only one supplier of commercial punches be dealt with. His standards should be made yours; in actuality this is what usually happens in large companies. Such commercial punches are available not only in round shapes, but also in other shapes including oblong, square, rectangular, and triangular.

For larger punches, which usually must be home-made, take into account that the outer "bark" must be removed from the steel bar. If possible, select such "net" sizes which are about $\frac{1}{8}$ in. smaller in diameter than the commercial tool steel bar sizes. The punch diameter should be $1\frac{3}{8}$ in. for a tool steel bar of $1\frac{1}{2}$ in.

For multiple punching when the component is punched with more than one die, all the holes punched in a given stamping or at least all the holes in a given die should be, if possible, identical in shape and size. If this is not possible, the number of different hole sizes and/or shapes should be reduced as much as possible.

case histories

PRACTICAL HINTS FOR FLAT BLANKS AND HOLES

In this chapter a few suggestions are presented which can help the designer to solve problems that may occur during the design of flat metal stampings.

A typical case is represented by washers for fasteners (screws, bolts, nuts, rivets, etc.). Washers are usually made by blanking round rings from sheet stock, and waste is normally high, ranging from 30 to 60 percent. By changing the shape to hexagonal, a semiscrapless design is created with a waste of less than 10 percent. In addition, the corner of a polygonal washer may be bent up to lock the hexagonal head of the bolt or the nut (see Appendix A).

In Figs. 6–1 and 6–2 the width of the fingers a and that of the canals b have been slightly changed so that they became equal to c and d (identical between them) as shown in Fig. 6–3. Consequently, the component can be produced with an almost scrapless strip layout with a material saving of almost 30 percent (see Fig. 6–4).

In another case, the workpiece has been designed according to Fig. 6–5 so that the corresponding strip will be as illustrated in Fig. 6–6 with .36 sq in. material used per piece. A change in the contour of the workpiece as shown in Fig. 6–7, results in a material savings of 33.3 percent of the original design (see Fig. 6–8).

Figs. 6–9 through 6–16 show several more blanks which have been redesigned for better stock utilization. In the case of Fig. 6–10, the next logical step would be a scrapless design, but in this specific case it was not possible because the scrapless design had a few limitations.

Fan blades for light duty, e.g., small refrigerator units, are made from sheet metal. Stiffening ribs in the blades give the necessary strength. The blade shown in Fig. 6–17 can be produced as follows:

1) Shear the strips
2) Blank the parts
3) Punch the holes
4) Form the rib and twist the blade.

The material used in this case is high. By redesigning, the part is made from coil material with practically no scrap (see Fig. 6–18). The production process is as follows:

1) The coil is cropped to correct length with the two ends suitably trimmed and shaped

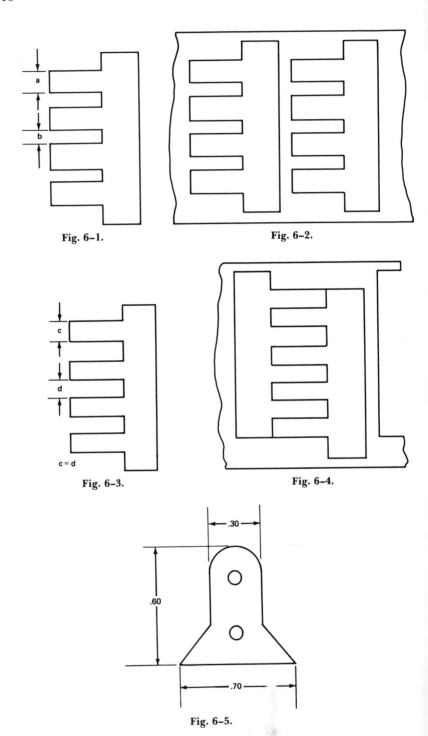

Fig. 6–1.

Fig. 6–2.

Fig. 6–3.

Fig. 6–4.

Fig. 6–5.

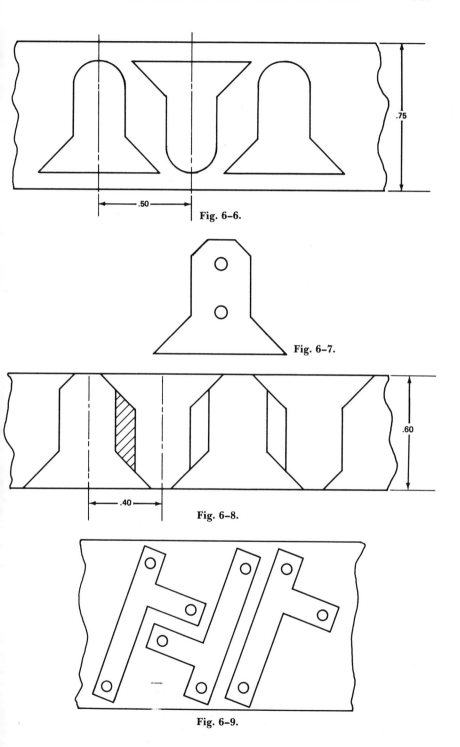

Fig. 6–6.

Fig. 6–7.

Fig. 6–8.

Fig. 6–9.

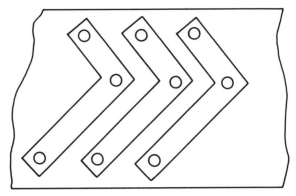

Fig. 6–10.

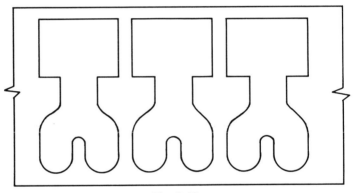

Fig. 6–11.

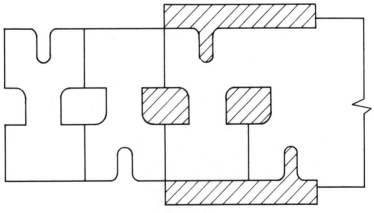

Fig. 6–12.

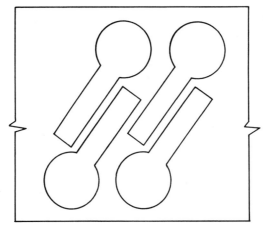

Fig. 6–13.

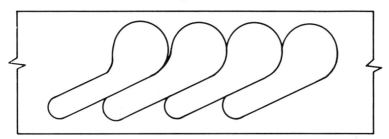

Fig. 6–14.

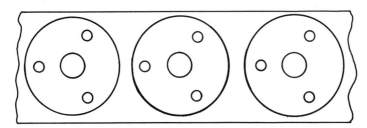

Fig. 6–15.

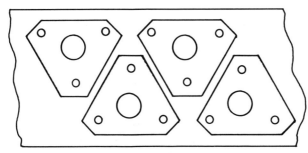

Fig. 6–16.

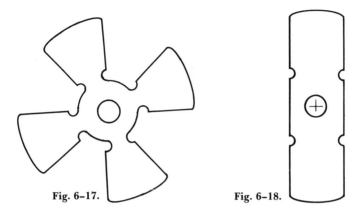

Fig. 6–17.   Fig. 6–18.

2) The four half-round notches near the center are punched

3) The two components in Fig. 6–19 are spot welded

4) The stiffening ribs are embossed and the blades twisted in the same operation.

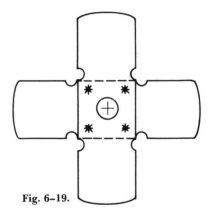

Fig. 6–19.

With the improved design there are some more operations to perform. However, these operations are simpler, and therefore, quicker and less expensive than the operations of the original design. Especially favorable is the elimination of the handling of the large sheets and the heavy strips. The material savings is more than 30 percent.

The blanks shown in Fig. 6–20 were produced from very thin steel sheet (.008 in.). The end point of the top in the workpieces had to be very sharp. Even if it were possible to make the tool with sharp cutting points, the duration of the sharpness would have been impractically short. In fact, satisfactory results cannot be guaranteed if the apex of the teeth form is less than .015 in. radius.

The problem has been solved satisfactorily by trimming the end point in two separate, intersecting operations. The tool built for this case is a two-station progressive die (see Fig. 6–21). At the first station the small round hole is punched, and another punch cuts one side of the strip. At the second station, another punch blanks out the finished stamping.

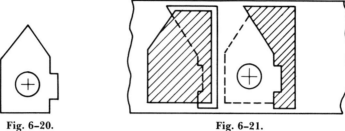

Fig. 6-20. Fig. 6-21.

Sometimes more money is spent on material and tooling in order to gain time and/or accuracy in assembly. When terminals are to be embedded in plastic moldings and the relative position of the metal stamping inserts is critical, the terminals are usually prepunched and held together with two side lists left after the stamping operation. After the plastic molding operation, the two side lists are simply removed by a proper shearing operation (see Figs. 6-22 and 6-23).

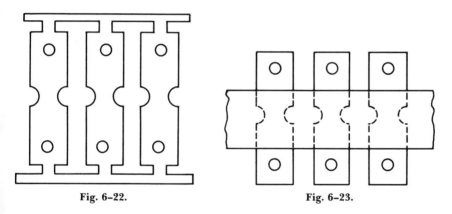

Fig. 6-22. Fig. 6-23.

If a hole *must* be punched close to the stamping edge or close to another punched hole, some special steps will have to be taken to avoid distortions or bulges in the workpiece. Four remedies are possible when punching a single hole that is twice the diameter of the stock thickness and is undesirably close to the edge of a flat stamping:

1) Increase the critical distance by shifting the hole. Displace it a little further away from the edge; or carry away the internal stamping edge from the hole.
2) Leave the hole where it is, but change the stamping profile by adding some metal in the form of an ear or tab around the hole, i.e., increase the blank size as shown in Fig. 6-24. If necessary, the superfluous metal may be trimmed or shaved away afterwards.
3) Leave the hole where it is, and open it toward the edge; i.e., transform the hole into an open slot as illustrated in Fig. 6-25
4) Drill the hole. This solution involves additional labor costs not found in the other remedies.

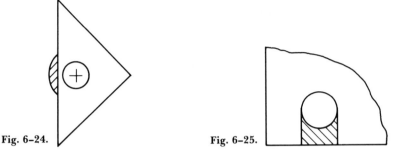

Fig. 6–24.   Fig. 6–25.

Flat stampings with multiple holes often have the additional problem of being too close to adjacent holes. The possible remedies are two:

1) Increase the distance between the holes by shifting one or both of them
2) Leave the holes where they are and join them, i.e., making one oblong or irregular, common aperture.

PRACTICAL HINTS FOR FORMED STAMPINGS

The principle about freedom of stamping shape design or modifications is also applied to formed and/or compound bent stampings. A typical case illustrates the idea. A part must be manufactured with a base which supports three holes in determined positions with respect to the base. The design shown in Fig. 6–26 produces too much scrap. Fig. 6–27 illustrates a design which al-

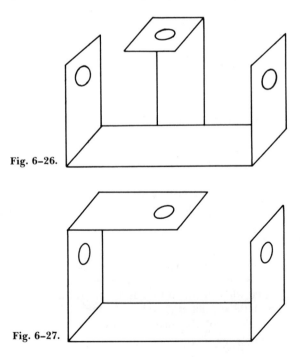

Fig. 6–26.

Fig. 6–27.

lows the use of simple shearing with a 100 percent material utilization factor, and simpler and therefore less expensive tooling.

An even more satisfactory arrangement is presented in the next example. Here two stampings are produced which form the two halves of a coupling for light duty. Fig. 6–28 illustrates the assembly with the corresponding two shafts.

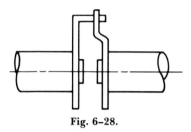

Fig. 6–28.

The strip layout with cutting edges using the corresponding progressive-type die that double shears with preliminary notchings and punchings is shown in Fig. 6–29. The finished stampings are shown in Figs. 6–30 and 6–31. The material is almost totally utilized in this case; the only unavoidable waste are

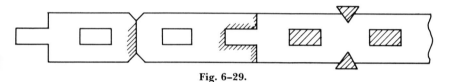

Fig. 6–29.

the punching slugs. However, these are not entirely lost because the scrap which would be created by notching out the slot of the female part of the coupling (see Fig. 6–30) becomes the nose of the male counterpart (see Fig. 6–31). A similar case is presented in Figs. 3–21 through 3–23. Here the slug punched out from the main stamping is used as a component for the assembly.

A slot, located near the bending zone of a component, will be deformed by

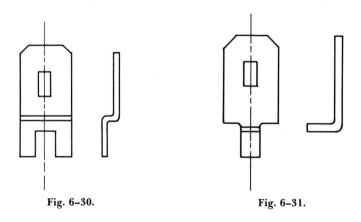

Fig. 6–30.   Fig. 6–31.

the bending operation (see Fig. 6–32). To compensate for this deformation, the original slot, in the flat before the bending operation, should be a shape that after the deformation has the desired contour and size. Before bending, the original form of the notch can be determined only by practical tests and trials.

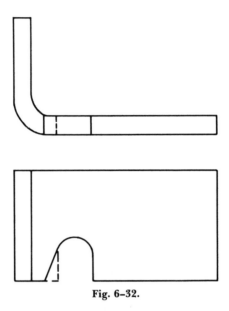

Fig. 6–32.

Foolproof Nesting of Blanks in Second Operation Dies

In bending, the burr side of the stampings must lay at the internal side of the bend. To insure that this is done whenever possible, the nesting of the flat blanks should be made foolproof. Some detail should be incorporated into the tool which makes it impossible to wrongly locate the blank or at least warn the operator so that he will not position the blank incorrectly. Warnings on the operation sheet or the tool are not satisfactory; they are ignored too often.

The foolproof or safety device consists usually of a simple pin or a specially shaped block, corresponding to slots or notches put in the right places, i.e., in the blank shape which makes it totally or partially unsymmetrical in the slots, notches, or around protruding tongs, ribs, tabs, etc. The foolproof device is located so that it clears only correctly positioned parts.

Unless the foolproofing pin does not participate actively and directly in close tolerance aligning of the workpieces, it is good practice to use rolled pins or groove pins. These do not require accurately drilled or reamed holes as do dowel pins. In every case, the foolproof device must be visible so the operator can instantly see the correct orientation of the blanks.

Fig. 6–33 illustrates a typical example. The part is aligned by its periphery, and a correctly located pin aligns the blank. Thus, the bending may be performed only in correct location with respect to the slot in the blank and the burr on the outer contour.

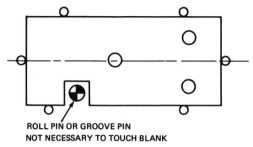

ROLL PIN OR GROOVE PIN
NOT NECESSARY TO TOUCH BLANK
Fig. 6-33.

To make symmetrical blanks foolproof, the parts must be made slightly unsymmetrical by making some special slot, notch, chamfer, etc. in some functionally unimportant portion of the blank contour. The figures below illustrate the most commonly used means for changing a symmetrical part to an unsymmetrical part:

Figs. 6-34 and 6-35 — Changing the blank dimensions

Fig. 6-36 — Trimming (cutting away) a corner of the blank contour

Fig. 6-37 — Chamfering a contour portion

Fig. 6-38 — Modifying the blank contour by off-setting a projection

Fig. 6-39 — Changing the shape of the blank contour

Figs. 6-40 and 6-41 — Increasing the width of one of the narrow slots

Fig. 6-42 — Punching a special off-set hole in the blank interior

Fig. 6-43 — Notching a half-hole or a rectangular slot in the blank periphery

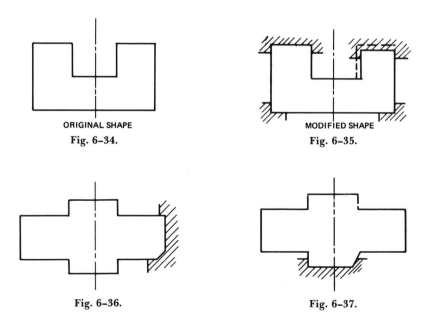

ORIGINAL SHAPE
Fig. 6-34.

MODIFIED SHAPE
Fig. 6-35.

Fig. 6-36.

Fig. 6-37.

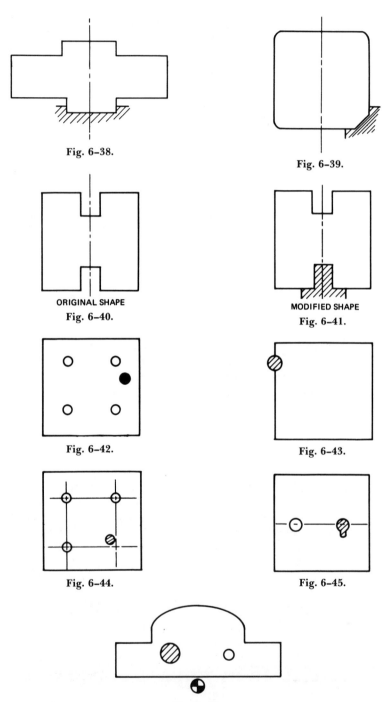

Fig. 6–38.

Fig. 6–39.

ORIGINAL SHAPE
Fig. 6–40.

MODIFIED SHAPE
Fig. 6–41.

Fig. 6–42.

Fig. 6–43.

Fig. 6–44.

Fig. 6–45.

Fig. 6–46.

Fig. 6–44 – Off-setting or shifting one of the functional holes
Fig. 6–45 – Changing the shape of the functional hole
Fig. 6–46 – Making one of the functional holes larger.
In case of high precision requirements, employ (1) multiple operations such as any double or triple method, etc., or (2) any reasonable combination among the methods shown in Figs. 6–34 through 6–46.

Twisting

Among the special forming operations, twisting must be mentioned. This consists of changing, by torsion, the relative angular position of portions of a body, without changing its axis (see Fig. 6–47). This operation may be performed either with special press tools, or with jigs or hand tools. Selection of a

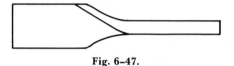

Fig. 6–47.

manufacturing method depends on quantities, tolerances, and other circumstances. The usual angle is 90 deg; however, any other value is possible.
Twisting is little known and little practiced. The designer should keep it in mind because sometimes the most economical solution of a given design problem consists of twisting a portion of the stamping.

PRACTICAL HINTS FOR DRAWN PARTS

In designing drawn workpieces, the following information may help to avoid production and tooling difficulties, to reduce manufacturing costs, and to solve technical or economical problems.
If lubricated blanks have the tendency to stick together, it is unavoidable that sometimes two blanks will be placed simultaneously in the tool. As a result, accidents, injuries to tools and machines, rejected components, etc. may occur, if such blanks are used in subsequent drawing operations. In order to prevent this trouble, a small nonconcentric protuberance or dimple may be stamped in the blanks when possible. The dimple may be stamped with a blanking punch that has a small tip, similar to a reduced pilot pin (see Fig. 6–48).
The open ends of shells are sometimes curled to both stiffen the part and to prevent injuries. Remember that outside curling is simpler, easier, and less expensive than inside curling.
High stresses exist in the top or open end of drawn shells, especially if made from comparatively thin stock. If the stresses are released with deep slots (see Fig. 6–49), or with windows located too near the top (see Fig. 6–50), the shells will distort. Slots should be very short (see Fig. 6–51), and windows located well away from the top edge (see Fig. 6–52).
Instead of a bulging operation, a composite construction built up from two comparatively easy drawn parts (see Fig. 6–53) is preferable.
In the edge of the rim of the drawn cup illustrated in Fig. 6–54, a through

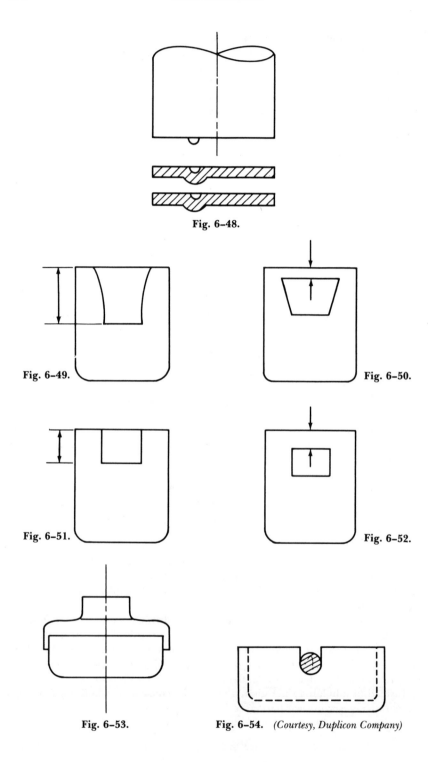

Fig. 6–48.

Fig. 6–49.

Fig. 6–50.

Fig. 6–51.

Fig. 6–52.

Fig. 6–53.

Fig. 6–54.   *(Courtesy, Duplicon Company)*

opening was needed for clearing a wire of a given diameter. In the original design, slots were milled at opposite sides of a fully drawn shell. Since the shape of the slot is unimportant, the cup design was changed so that the slot milling operation was eliminated. First, a round blank with two cut-away segments was considered (see Fig. 6–55). The blank was produced with a round blanking die

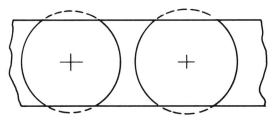

Fig. 6–55. *(Courtesy, Duplicon Company)*

from a strip narrower than the blank diameter. This blank was supposed to give a drawn shell according to Fig. 6–56. In this way, the overall cost would have been reduced considerably by decreasing every cost detail: tooling, labor, and stock. However, tests showed that the parts came out with stretched ears as illustrated in Fig. 6–57. So a blank had to be developed that was fully blanked from the strip (see Fig. 6–58). Even in this case, an overall savings resulted because supplementary machining was avoided.

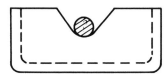

Fig. 6–56. *(Courtesy, Duplicon Company)*

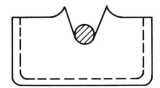

Fig. 6–57. *(Courtesy, Duplicon Company)*

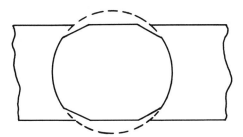

Fig. 6–58. *(Courtesy, Duplicon Company)*

The next case involving junction boxes and similar products has a universal value. At the bottom edge some holes must be designed for the passage of the electric wires. It is customary for designers to specify well-shaped apertures according to Fig. 6–59.

This design requires the holes to be punched after the drawing of the box.

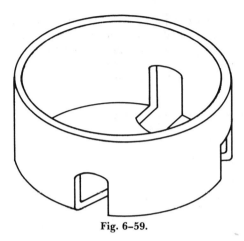

Fig. 6–59.

Instead of such a design, the following procedure is suggested. At the right locations punch simple round holes in the flat blank before the drawing operation. During the drawing process, these holes will be slightly deformed (see Fig. 6–60), but this will not interfere with introducing the leads into the box. Savings are realized by eliminating multiple operations.

Fig. 6–61 represents a case where the drawing operation can be eliminated. According to the original specification, this workpiece was to be drawn and

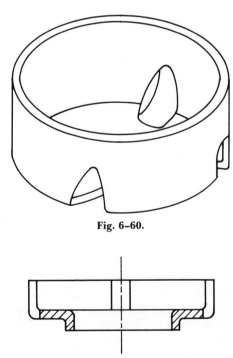

Fig. 6–60.

Fig. 6–61.

afterward slit with a thin circular saw. Instead of such a complicated and expensive procedure, the four notches are first made in the flat blank (see Fig. 6–62). Instead of drawing a cylinder, now four segments are bent upward in arcs, and the small collar or boss is formed downward with the same tool in the same operation. Thus, a costly multiple machining operation of slitting is totally eliminated, and the chief tooling became simpler and less expensive.

The workpiece shown in Fig. 6–63 is similar. With the original design, a cylindrical shell was drawn, and then the side walls were notched four times. The delicate tooling and the troublesome operation were replaced by the following procedure: a lower, cylindrical shell with a flange was drawn. The flange was then trimmed with an almost normal multiple-notching tool (see Fig. 6–64). Finally, the remaining ears were turned upward. The production

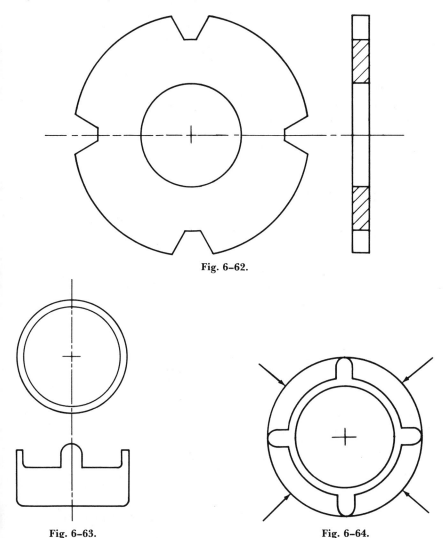

Fig. 6–62.

Fig. 6–63.   Fig. 6–64.

techniques were later modified even further. A specially shaped flat blank (see Fig. 6–65) was shallow-drawn, and the workpiece was ready with this one operation. Thus, two operations were eliminated with corresponding reductions in tooling and labor cost. In addition, less stock was needed.

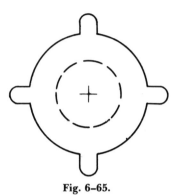

Fig. 6–65.

To produce the part shown in Fig. 6–66, flat strips of sheet metal are simply formed and assembled by spot welding, and then a central hole is punched in the bottom. This part replaces a drawn cup in which four sectors had to be punched out in the bottom. Considerable savings of material, labor, and tooling were realized with the fabricated design.

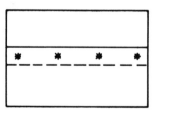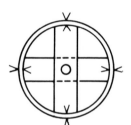

Fig. 6–66.

Aldo L. Coen introduced a totally new concept in the manufacturing of light duty perforated basket-like drawn parts. A typical application of this principle are speaker housings for loudspeakers. The new idea consists of using a blank of the same size as the finished housing, punching strategically located kidney-shaped slots in it, and then forming the part into the required three-dimensional speaker housing shape. In the last operation, the slots are enlarged, assuming a diamond-shaped lace pattern which is functionally necessary for unhindered air flow in both directions.

The advantages of the expanded metal design over the conventional method of drawn sheet metal parts may be summed up as follows:

    1) Reduced raw material costs: (a) less stock is used, (b) commercial quality sheet metal can be employed instead of special drawing quality steel

    2) Increased production rates: (a) fewer operations, (b) simpler operations

3) Avoidance of internal stresses which are set up in drawn parts by severe plastic flow of metal during the drawing process

4) Flexibility of design in that a forming tool is very easily adapted to different forming depths.

MISCELLANEOUS CASE HISTORIES

Embedding Metal Stamping Inserts

A metal insert may be embedded in plastic or another metal with a lower point of fusion while the other metal or plastic is in a liquid or plastic state. After the surrounding material becomes solid, an integral bond is created between the two parts. The insert is firmly held in place because the plastic or metal shrinks and has a faster thermal contraction rate than the insert metal.

One of the most important features in the design of a metal insert is its anchorage. In any type of insert it is necessary to design some kind of gripping or holding anchorage to prevent the possibility of pulling the insert out under axial load, and to prevent turning or radial movement under torsional load. The shrinkage of the anchoring material alone is not always sufficient to guarantee these goals.

According to the type and shape of the insert, but chiefly according to the kind and intensity of the corresponding loads, the following simple, inexpensive anchorage methods are commonly employed:

1) The stamping is shaped with a head (see Fig. 6–67)

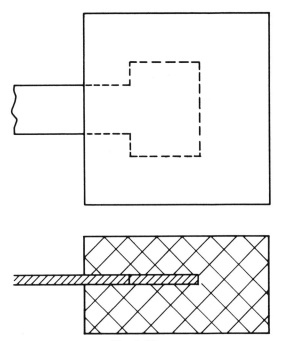

Fig. 6–67.

2) Sometimes the stamping has a functional shape which lends itself naturally as an excellent anchorage (see Fig. 6–68)

3) Punched holes (see Figs. 6–69 and 6–70)

4) Notched slots (see Fig. 6–71)

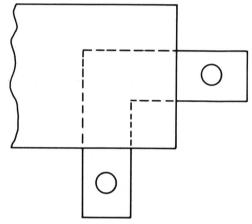

Fig. 6–68.

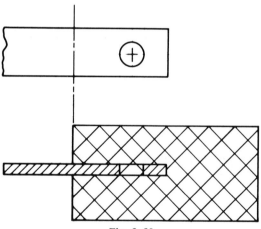

Fig. 6–69.

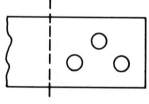

Fig. 6–70.

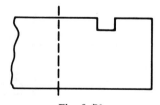

Fig. 6–71.

5) Extruded holes offer higher anchorage strength than simple punched holes (see Fig. 2–16)
6) Protrusions are used sometimes for moderate loads (see Fig. 2–54)
7) Beads or ribs (see Fig. 3–54)
8) Tabs or legs (see Fig. 6–72). Tabs should be bent more than 90 deg to achieve a strong wedge action.

Obviously, the metal insert must be surrounded by the other material so that the two materials will not separate during cooling. If it is imperative to leave the insert at the outside, then the joint must be shaped so that eventually the other material will grip the insert anyway (see Fig. 6–73).

Inserts located flush with or anywhere on the outer surface, may be anchored as follows:

1) Countersunk holes (see Fig. 6–74)
2) Shear-formed tabs (see Figs. 2–26 and 2–27) always at an acute angle

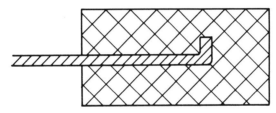

Fig. 6–72.

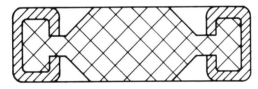

Fig. 6–73.

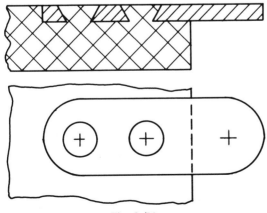

Fig. 6–74.

3) Extruded holes (see Fig. 6–75)
4) Special shaping of the whole stamping (Fig. 6–76)
5) Tubular and drawn shell inserts are anchored by light knurling, by flattening, crimping, nicking, flanging, or by other means according to the circumstances.

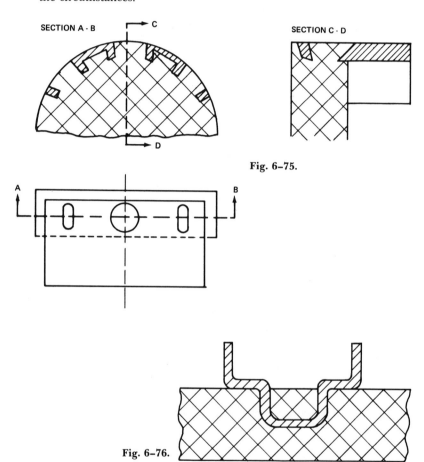

SECTION A - B

SECTION C - D

Fig. 6–75.

Fig. 6–76.

Production of Short Tube Lengths

In cents per pound seamless steel tubing cost much more than common cold rolled steel sheets. So it is worthwhile to consider the possibilities offered by producing short tube lengths with press tool methods. Savings in cost and in time are realized by proceeding to draw a cylindrical flangeless shell of correct dimensions and simply punching out the bottom. The body of the shell represents the required length of tubing.

On the other hand, short pieces of tubing may be made very inexpensively by rolling a piece of flat sheet metal into a cylindrical shape and butt-welding the seam afterward. Such a design is practical even in those cases where small flanges at one or both ends are needed (see Fig. 6–77).

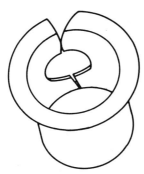

Fig. 6-77.

An Unusual Assembly Method

A score of known fastening methods are used to join two sheet metal parts or to join a sheet metal stamping to a cast, forged, or otherwise machined or a plastic part. However, sometimes it is not possible nor practical to employ any of the standard assembly methods. This often happens when a part is produced by some other manufacturing process and is redesigned for production as a sheet metal stamping. To avoid high transformation costs and trouble, certain existing conditions must be maintained unaltered.

For instance, a company decided to change from machine manufacturing of levers to metal stamping of levers. The levers were originally assembled with their counterparts by threading the machined lever-ends, and screwing them into tapped holes in the counterparts. Redesign of the part involved stamping the body into a channel shape, while the tip was rolled into a round shape. This short end was then threaded with a special threading die which produces the required threads (see Fig. 6-78).

The sheet metal gage was selected so that it is the maximum thickness and yet could be formed into a round shape on a comparatively small diameter. The stiffness of the steel sheet was increased by coldworking during the forming process and gave excellent strength characteristics to the part.

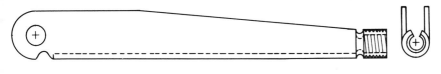

Fig. 6-78. *(Courtesy, Duplicon Company)*

COMPOSITE METAL STAMPING DESIGNS

Many individual stampings have been designed originally as one-piece jobs, and then converted into subassemblies composed of two or more parts properly joined together. There are several reasons for doing this:

1) To avoid trouble with tooling caused by intricate shape of stamping and/or high accuracy requirements

2) To reduce tooling costs caused by complicated stamping shapes and/or stamping size

3) To reduce labor and stock costs due to size and/or intricateness of stamping (low stock utilization factors)

4) To avoid metal flow problems

5) To solve certain design problems such as strength, performance, and special requirements through combinations of components made from different kinds of material

6) To make easier servicing, especially assembly and replacement of worn parts

7) To effect savings through standardization of product components, etc.

In this section a few characteristic cases taken from actual practice are presented. These examples illustrate the advantages which may be realized through judicious application of composite construction of stampings.

It is often convenient to divide a large stamping into two halves and to join them together by some adequate method. For instance, car body parts can be improved considerably if the stampings are welded together from two halves (see Figs. 6–79 and 6–80).

An assembled composite design sometimes is favorable and advantageous not only in large workpieces but also in comparatively small parts. Paper fasteners (see Figs. 4–63 through 4–65) used for holding together papers, letters, etc. are in this category. By making them in composite design, instead of in one single piece, material savings of about 25 percent have been effected with little increase in labor and tooling costs (see Figs. 4–63 through 4–65).

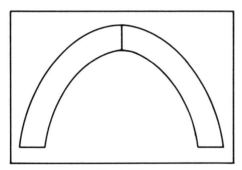

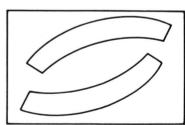

Fig. 6–79.   Fig. 6–80.

Many times the properties of the stock (chiefly ductility and work-hardening rate) do not allow one-piece designs. For instance, in Fig. 6–81 the simultaneous double cup draw plus U-bending would likely provoke too much stretching causing tearing of the stock. The design shown in Fig. 6–82 avoids this trouble. Figs. 6–83 and 6–84 show the solution for excessively large flanges for tubings. Similar solutions are sometimes sought to avoid distortions in lithographed stock which must be drawn or formed. In certain cases lapped joints may compensate for close tolerances in welded constructions. Lap joints make it possible to hold critical dimensions (see Fig. 6–85).

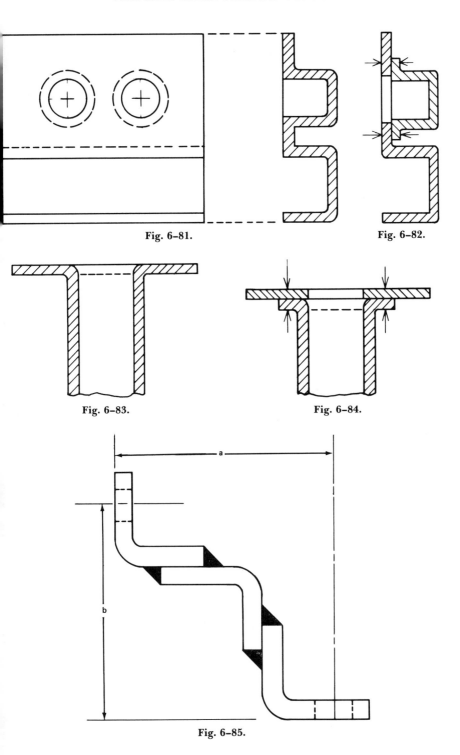

Fig. 6–81.

Fig. 6–82.

Fig. 6–83.

Fig. 6–84.

Fig. 6–85.

It is not convenient to make round stampings which require hubs in one-piece construction. Such machine elements as gears, pulley wheels, and fans are best made in sections and assembled by welding, brazing, staking, press fit, etc. Fig. 6–86 illustrates a wheel which is composed of two identical drawn parts and a machined hub, all brazed together to form the desired product. A pulley design is shown in Fig. 6–87, in which a formed stamping is spot-welded to a machined hub.

Simple male and female cylindrical gages are often made very successfully in composite design. Male gages are provided with a handle; the actual gage is usually a drawn simple or double walled shell heat treated, ground, lapped, and chromium-plated (see Figs. 6–88 through 6–90 and also Fig. 2–20).

The composite design often permits ingenious solutions of seemingly difficult problems by assembling two or more parts from different kinds of materials. By taking advantage of the properties of each material excellent constructions may result.

A closure for perfume bottles has been made in sectional construction by joining an external octagonal drawn brass cap for esthetics and an internal aluminum drawn and threaded shell for the actual fastening.

A special case of the combination design is represented by the intimate joining of two different metals or alloys which are then stamped, machined, etc. to form components of many kinds. With these clad metals very interesting and unusual requirements may be met, such as increasing resistance against corrosion, heat, abrasion, chemical reactions, etc. A special field of application are thermostat metals where two metals having different coefficients of thermal expansion are rolled together.

The cladding must not be necessarily integral; it may be only partial. For the production of certain electrical contacts, small silver strips are rolled into the parent copper strips, and the contacts are blanked out of the partially clad material (see Fig. 6–91).

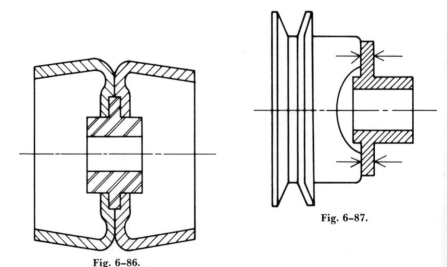

Fig. 6–87.

Fig. 6–86.

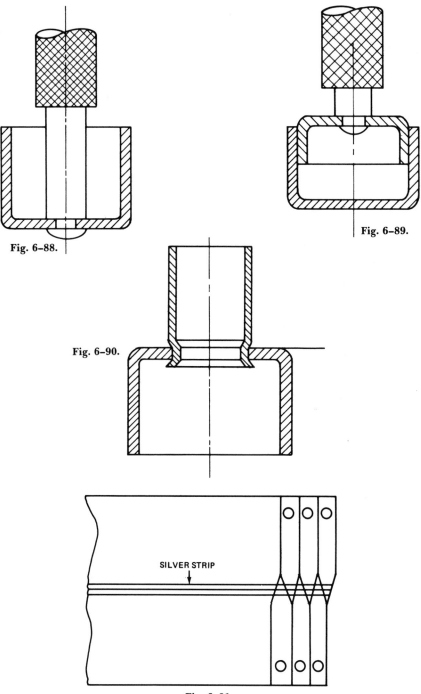

Fig. 6–88.

Fig. 6–89.

Fig. 6–90.

SILVER STRIP

Fig. 6–91.

CONVERSION FROM OTHER MANUFACTURING PROCESSES
TO STAMPING TECHNIQUE

Conversion of Cast Workpieces

The component shown in Fig. 6–92 was originally die cast, then machined, and finally finished. The stamped version (see Fig. 6–93) requires only two operations: blanking and punching in a common progressive die plus channel forming. The considerable savings in labor and raw material compensated at a very low quantity for the difference in tooling costs. The outer contour of

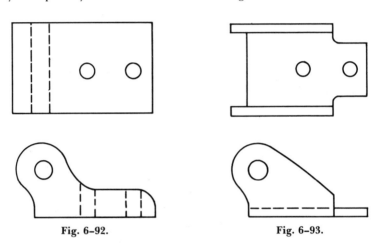

Fig. 6–92.   Fig. 6–93.

the flat blank has been slightly changed to a curvilinear instead of straight end to get a better strip layout. This produces a more favorable stock utilization factor. Fig. 6–94 shows how a slight change, which does not affect the function or strength of the part, decreases material waste.

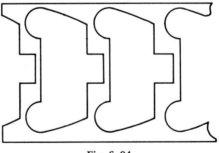

Fig. 6–94.

The change from a cast bearing sleeve (see Fig. 6–95) to a stamping (see Fig. 6–96) not only reduced raw material and labor but also reduced the space needed for the part. Consequently, the housing in which the bearing sleeve is located became smaller, lighter, and less expensive.

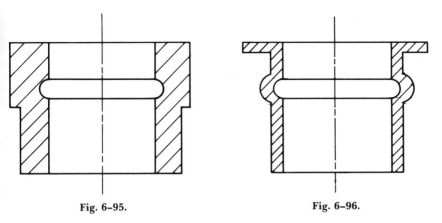

Fig. 6–95.   Fig. 6–96.

Instead of a complicated casting (see Fig. 6–97) which involves a lot of machining, a three-part assembly is brazed together from two stampings and a piece of tubing (see Fig. 6–98).

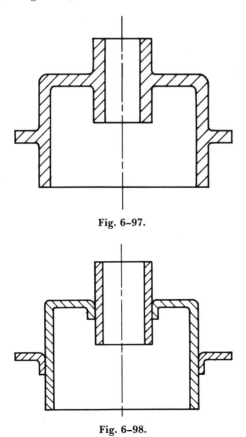

Fig. 6–97.

Fig. 6–98.

Conversion of Machined Components

Originally, the component shown in Fig. 6–99 had been produced by a considerable amount of milling, drilling, and other operations, from cold rolled flat steel. Since this workpiece was required in comparatively high quantities, it was converted to stamping production. After slightly changing its outer contour, the component (see Fig. 6–100) was produced in an inexpensive scrapless design by a multistage progressive die that stamped out two stampings at each press-stroke.

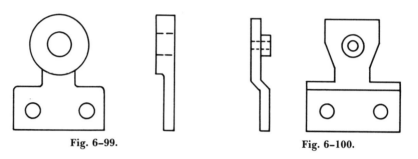

Fig. 6–99.   Fig. 6–100.

Investigation of the machined part illustrated in Fig. 6–101 showed that it could be replaced by a simple tapered washer (see Fig. 6–102). The part was shaped in one operation with a blanking punch and ground with the proper taper. Considerable savings in material and labor were realized in this case. The old design was machined from a solid block; the replacement stamping is made from sheet metal. The material saved was about 87 percent; the cost of labor saved was about 92 percent. Reduction in assembly labor of about 46 percent was realized.

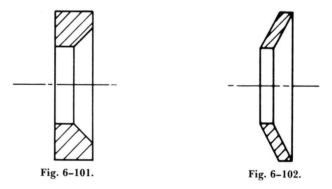

Fig. 6–101.   Fig. 6–102.

Instead of milling the hollow shape needed for guiding a sliding counterpart from solid metal (see Fig. 6–103), a stamping (see Fig. 6–104) from sheet metal is employed in this case. The savings in stock and in labor are substantial.

Parts manufactured on a screw-machine (see Fig. 6–105) are often easily replaced by drawn and further processed sheet metal stampings (Fig. 6–106). Even where comparatively low quantities are concerned, the stampings are cheaper than the corresponding machined parts.

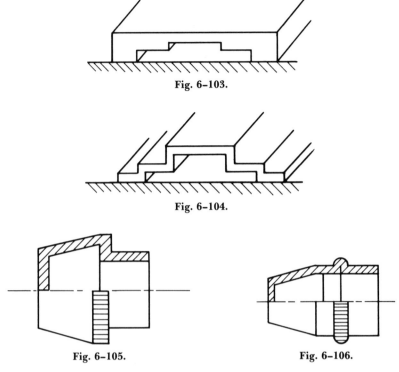

Fig. 6–103.

Fig. 6–104.

Fig. 6–105.   Fig. 6–106.

If a tube with a stop collar is machined from a thick walled tubing, the material waste is rather high; if processed from a piece of thin walled tubing with the stop collar being produced by a simple beading operation, no material is wasted (see Figs. 6–107 through 6–109). Also labor is notably reduced.

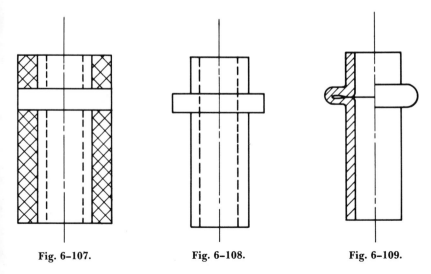

Fig. 6–107.   Fig. 6–108.   Fig. 6–109.

Conversion of Assembled Components

An assembly made up from two round spacers and a yoke (see Fig. 6–110) can be replaced by a simple stamping from flat steel (see Fig. 6–111). Excellent savings in material, labor, and assembly costs are achieved through this design.

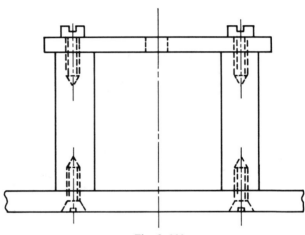

Fig. 6–110.

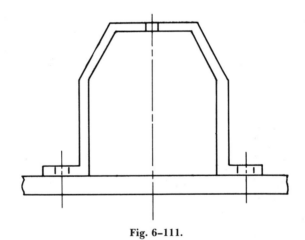

Fig. 6–111.

An actuating lever for a mechanism was made with a bushing staked to a flat handle (see Fig. 6–112). The part was redesigned so that it could be stamped in one piece and the assembly operation eliminated (see Fig. 6–113).

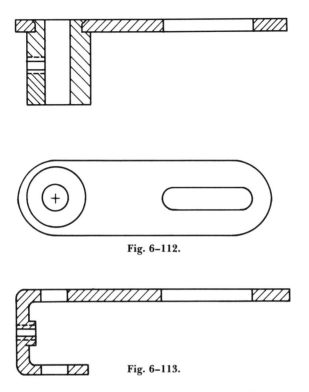

Fig. 6–112.

Fig. 6–113.

COMBINATION AMONG MACHINING AND PRESS OPERATIONS

One of the basic rules of machine or component design consists of designing the part or parts to conform to the production requirements of the intended corresponding manufacturing process. In fact, more or less marked differences in the shape and general design of components exist depending upon the manufacturing process to be used.

Usually, a rather sharp line separates the machining operations from press operations. While sheets and plates are reserved commonly for press tools, all other forms of stock are processed normally in machine tools. However, from time to time cases occur where components have such characteristics that they possess the combined convenient features of differently processed workpieces. In this section a few typical case histories concerning the production of workpieces by both machining and pressworking methods are shown.

Fig. 6–114 shows a rather common example. It is a terminal for a plug receptacle that is made from round copper stock cut to length. One end is swaged, and in this flattened portion two holes are punched. One hole is for tapping to fasten the lead, and the other hole is for alignment.

Fig. 6–115 illustrates another part where a single slot is opened by means of a very simple tool without a die plate. On the other hand, the safety fuse

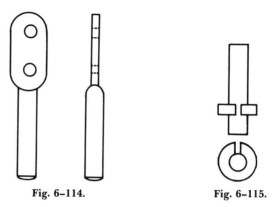

Fig. 6-114.   Fig. 6-115.

parts of Fig. 6-116 whose turned blank is presented in Fig. 6-117 needs a notching tool with somewhat sophisticated, elaborated, and special design with movable die plate sections.

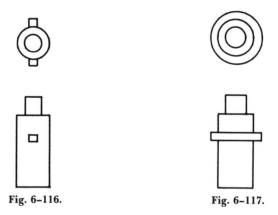

Fig. 6-116.   Fig. 6-117.

Obviously, punching a hole in a workpiece is much cheaper than drilling one. Nevertheless, in a few cases holes are drilled not only in machined or cast workpieces but even in sheet metal stampings. The chief reasons for this procedure may be summed up in the following points:

1) If the holes to be opened in the part are too small in relation to stock thickness (heavy stock) (see Fig. 2-4), it is recommended that prick punches be provided which during the blanking of the parts mark the correct position of the holes to be drilled afterward (see Fig. 6-118). To get the double advantage of more economical production and greater accuracy, it is recommended that the prick punches be put in the blanking

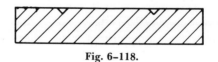

Fig. 6-118.

punch bottom; of course, in correct location with respect to blank outer contour.

2) For those cases in which the total quantity of parts is very low, economical consideration may advise not to provide special, separate punching dies, but to drill the holes, even if their size in relation to stock thickness is all right for punching.

3) In formed stampings, if some hole must be opened too near to the bending zone, it is a good practice not to punch the hole in the flat blanks but to drill them after the forming operation. Greater accuracy is achieved in this way.

Milling of stampings is also a rather common practice. Ordinary key blanks are slotted by the millions. Teeth are hobbed on stamped blank peripheries of partial gear segments, as shown in Fig. 6–119. Delicate, very accurate contour details of stampings, especially if made from comparatively heavy stock, are often finished by milling. In other cases, stamping portions are finished by broaching and sometimes by grinding.

The last case is interesting and is believed to be unique. A customer asked for a comparatively simple stamping as shown in Fig. 6–120. It is an L-shaped sheet metal part ($\frac{1}{16}$ in. thick) with one of the legs *roughened*. The part is a com-

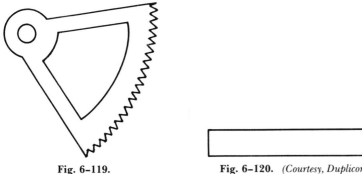

Fig. 6–119.   **Fig. 6–120.** *(Courtesy, Duplicon Company)*

ponent for a folding machine and works in combination with another similar part having a smoother surface. It is used to grip pieces of fabric to transport them from one position to another.

Normally, customers ask for smooth surfaces, but to roughen a surface meant something new. After considering a few possibilities, it was decided to machine the surface in question. The results were highly satisfactory, both from the performance and the economical standpoints. The surface of the stamping leg was simply knurled. A simple workpiece holding fixture was made and put into the vise of a standard shaper. After locking the toolpost to prevent swinging, a standard knurling tool as used currently in lathe work was inserted. After a couple of strokes, the diamond shaped knurling tool left the stamping roughened to the customer's specifications.

appendix A

Appendix A describes in detail two important types of metal stampings — stop plates and shafts.

Stop Plates for Locking Nuts and Bolts

When a screw-nut or bolt-nut assembly works under constant load, the self-locking feature of the standard triangular threads is sufficient to prevent unwanted loosening of the assembly. However, in many applications on machinery, tools, instruments, equipment, etc., fastening screws are subjected to variable loads. Oscillating and suddenly changing loads, shocks, impacts, vibrations, and other forces can produce elastic elongations and thus defeat the self-locking action with consequent unscrewing of the assembly. The same phenomenon may result from cyclic changes of temperature, corrosion, or simple shrinkage of the workpiece, e.g., if made from wood. Screws and nuts must, in some way, be safely secured against loosening caused by variable loads and stresses.

There are a number of solutions to the problem. The technique is empirical, but based upon personal judgment and experience. The magnitude and characteristics of the loads in question, the properties of the materials employed in the assembly components, and the probable consequences of loosening are major considerations; e.g., in vehicles, automobiles, and airplanes loosening may result in the loss of human life. The best locking method is determined to meet the unique requirements of each particular application.

There are many locking methods. Metal stampings as an auxiliary locking means are presented here. The case histories are from actual practice. They are classified in two groups: (1) reusable indefinitely, and (2) permanent. To the first group belong those designs that will be disassembled and reassembled again any number of times and where, upon reassembly, the same original locking conditions must be automatically reestablished without any reworking of parts.

To the second group belong those designs where the assembly is never to be dismounted. The components cannot be disassembled without difficulty and only after one or more components is damaged or even destroyed.

Locking Methods — Reusable Indefinitely. Stop-plates or keys of many kinds are employed with great success; their design is determined by workpiece and general working characteristics.

153

1) The simplest form is a small bracket made from steel sheet screwed on the workpiece so that the vertical leg of the bracket leans against one of the nut-faces after the nut is properly tightened on the bolt (see Fig. A–1)

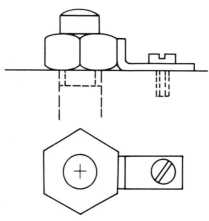

Fig. A-1.

2) The stop plate in Fig. A–2 is made from thick steel sheet and holds the nut or the hexagonal head of a bolt on two sides. This stop plate has an additional design feature which may be employed also in any other type of stop plate. The notches in the holding surface correspond to a 12 sided polygon instead of the six sides of a hexagonal bolt head or nut. Such a design permits 12 working positions instead of only six, and thus a much finer adjustment is possible for the tightening screws.

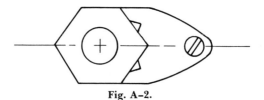

Fig. A-2.

3) Increasing the number of sides held by the plate to four makes the locking action safer (see Fig. A–3)

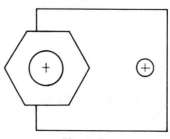

Fig. A-3.

4) Of course, a stop plate that completely surrounds the six sides is the safest (see Fig. A–4). Sometimes the hole is not hexagonal but has 12 sides (dodecagonal) analogous to the design of Fig. A–2.

5) For greatest safety, it is good practice to provide for the fastening of the stop plate itself, using two screws instead of only one (see Fig. A–5).

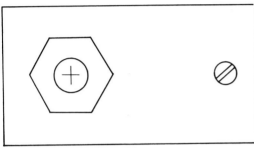

Fig. A–4.

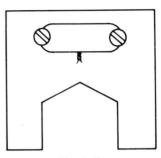

Fig. A–5.

6) Any of the above designs can be employed for pairs of nuts (see Fig. A–6) thus saving time, labor, and material in the construction of stop plates. Of course, the two screws must be located reasonably near to each other.

As may be seen from the reported examples, the outer contour of the stop plates is practically immaterial: it may be round, elongated, rectangular, irregular, etc.

In every case, both the bolt-head and the nut should be locked with a stop plate.

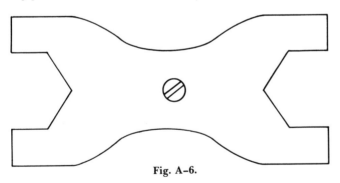

Fig. A–6.

7) The next stop plate designs are somewhat more elaborate. In the first case shown in Fig. A–7, two flaps or tabs are bent along two sides, after tightening the assembly. The second case (see Fig. A–8) is rather simple. In the rectangularly shaped stop plate, a slit is made along which the outer part of the stop plate is bent upward.

8) The design of Fig. A–9 is analogous to the design of Fig. A–8 with the difference that here the tab is open.

Permanent Locking Methods. There are several types of stop plates which are used in the shape of large washers. They are prevented from turning by

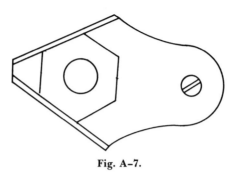

Fig. A–7.

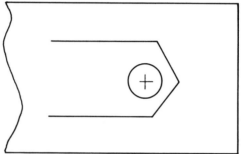

Fig. A–8.

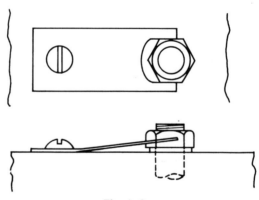

Fig. A–9.

some suitable means (see point 3 below). In turn, they impede the corresponding nut or bolt head from working loose by a bent tab or lug which is formed after tightening of the assembly. For dismounting the assembly, the bent tabs must be straightened. And if this operation is performed several times, the lugs break away. Therefore, this kind of locking device should be used only in permanent assemblies.

There is a great variety of such stop-plate-washers as illustrated in the corresponding sketches which illustrate the most commonly employed types.

Their chief characteristics are presented as follows:
1) They may be designed for one or two bolts (or nuts)
2) Their outer shape may be round, rectangular, rhomboidal, elongated; with or without external and/or internal additions (tabs) and respective notches (see Figs. A–10 through A–30 and Figs. A–1 through A–6)

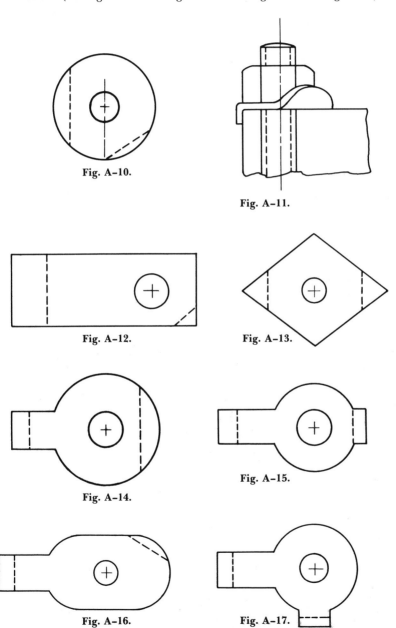

Fig. A–10.

Fig. A–11.

Fig. A–12.

Fig. A–13.

Fig. A–14.

Fig. A–15.

Fig. A–16.

Fig. A–17.

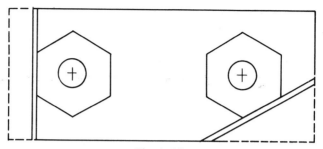

Fig. A-18.

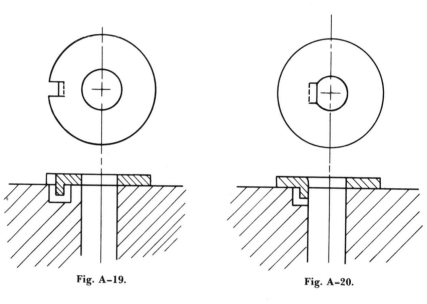

Fig. A-19.   Fig. A-20.

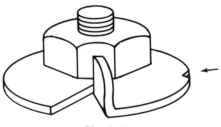

Fig. A-21.

3) The self-immobilization may be effected by several means, such as:
   a. Forcing the edge into the soft workpiece or into a previously drilled hole (see Fig. A-21)
   b. Bending against the workpiece edge (see Figs. A-13 and A-24)
   c. Leaning against a shoulder in the workpiece (see Fig. A-22)

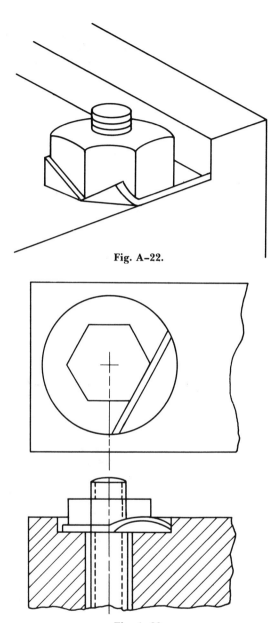

Fig. A-22.

Fig. A-23.

d. Introducing a lanced portion into a hole drilled in the workpiece (see Figs. A-19 and A-20)
e. Putting an eccentric hole in a round disc, and locating the disc in a matching offset recess in the workpiece (see Fig. A-23)
f. Milling longitudinal flats or slots on the bolt threads which match

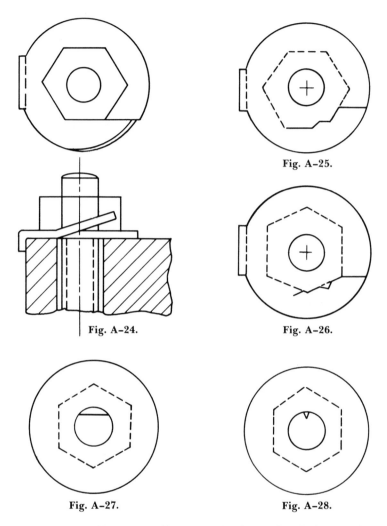

Fig. A-25.

Fig. A-24.

Fig. A-26.

Fig. A-27.   Fig. A-28.

corresponding protruding noses in the washer hole (see Figs. A-28
and A-29)

  g. Double-plates do not need any special device for self-immobilization

4) The locking action may be performed by:

  a. Bending up a right angle tab, flat against a side of the hexagon, a
standard practice

  b. Bending up a right angle split edge edgewise against a side of the
hexagon (see Fig. A-21)

  c. Bending up a split tab along the side of the hexagon (see Figs. A-24
and A-25). The design of Figs. A-25 and A-26 allow for a finer adjustment in the tightening of the nut; in fact, while the design of Fig.
A-24 demands steps of $\frac{1}{6}$ of a turn, those designs in Figs. A-25 and
A-26 permit steps of $\frac{1}{12}$ of a turn.

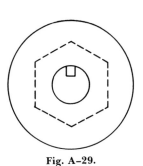

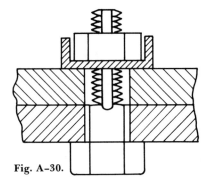

Fig. A–29.   Fig. A–30.

Shafts

Substituting hollow, drawn workpieces for solid dowel pins, rivets, short shafts, and similar machine elements is surprisingly little practiced, although careful application can result in savings in weight, material, and labor. The actual savings are generally 25 to 50 percent in weight, 30 to 70 percent in stock, and 50 to 80 percent in labor costs.

The design for such applications usually proceed as follows. The basic formulas for our considerations are to be found in any standard engineering handbook dealing with strength of materials. Taking into consideration a solid shaft as shown in Fig. A–31 with a diameter of d and a hollow shaft with an outside diameter of D and an inside diameter of d_1 (see Fig. A–32), the respective sections of modulus (moments of resistance) are:

$$Z_{\text{full shaft}} = .098d^3 \tag{A-1}$$

$$Z_{\text{hollow shaft}} = .098\frac{D^4 - d_1^4}{D} \tag{A-2}$$

If a full shaft must be replaced with a hollow shaft, then Eq. (A–2) must be made equal to Eq. (A–1). Thus:

$$.098d^3 = .098\frac{D^4 - d_1^4}{D}$$
$$d^3 = \frac{D^4 - d_1^4}{D} \tag{A-3}$$

Eq. (A–3) is the definitive equation for our calculations. Taking, for instance, an allowance of 20 percent for diameter increase (a reasonable value), Eq. (A–3) is transformed in this fashion:

$$d^3 = \frac{(1.2d)^4 - d_1^4}{1.2d}$$
$$d_1^4 = 2.07d^4 - 1.2d^4$$
$$d_1 = .96d$$

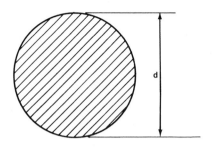

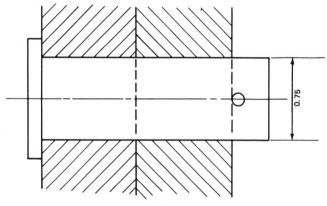

Fig. A-31.

The stock thickness for the hollow part is calculated simply and easily:

$$T = \frac{D - d_1}{2}$$

Since in case $D = 1.2d$ and $d_1 = .96d$

$$T = \frac{1.2d - .96d}{2}$$

$$T = .12d$$

For other diameter increase allowances, see the graph in Fig. A-33 where the ratios between d_1 and d and between T and d, respectively, are plotted for the usual range of values.

Once the dimensions of the hollow part (D, d_1 and T) are established, calculate the corresponding savings in weight. This is inversely proportional with the x magnitude of the diameter increase and corresponding wall thickness reduction.

Also, the formulas for the comparison of areas are taken from standard engineering handbooks:

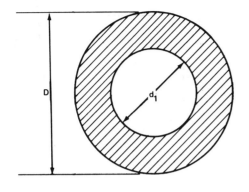

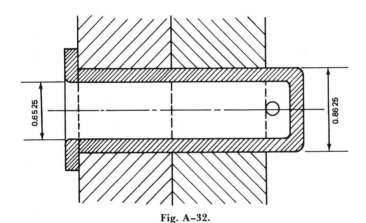

Fig. A-32.

$$A_{\text{full shaft}} \quad = .7854d^2 \qquad\qquad (A-4)$$

$$A_{\text{hollow shaft}} = .7854(D^2 - d_1^2) \qquad\qquad (A-5)$$

Taking again our former example with $D : d = 1.2$ ratio, the cross-sectional area of the hollow shaft will be:

$$A_{\text{hollow shaft}} = .7854[(1.2d)^2 - (.96d)^2]$$
$$= .7854(1.44d^2 - .92d^2)$$
$$= .7854(.52d^2)$$
$$= .4084d^2$$

Thus if the weight of the shell bottom is neglected, there is a weight savings of 48 percent with respect to the full shaft. For other $D : d$ ratios, consult the graph which shows the corresponding savings in percent for the usual diameter increase ranges.

A practical example taken from actual experience illustrates the procedure outlined above. The dowel pin of Fig. A-31 has been replaced by the drawn

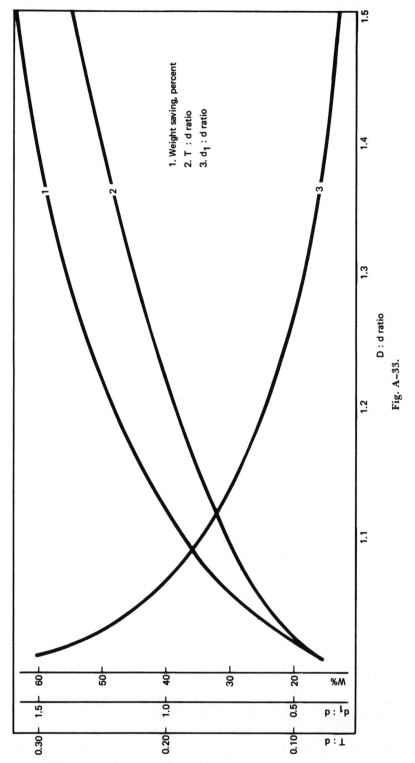

Fig. A–33.

shell of Fig. A–32. The dimensions of the latter have been determined to allow a diameter increase of 15 percent, as follows:

$$D = 1.15 \times .75 = .8625$$
$$d_1 = .87 \times .75 = .6525$$
$$T = (.8625 - .6525) : 2 = .105$$

(Gage No. 12) Weight saving = 44 percent.

appendix B

COST ESTIMATING OF METAL STAMPINGS

Pressworking of metals is based mostly on personal, practical experience, imagination, intuition, and ingenuity — not on cold, scientific, numerically expressed facts. It is interesting to note that one of the most characteristically unscientific activities in the pressworking of metals is the cost estimating of stampings.

The total cost of a metal stamping is composed of several cost details. The chief determining factor is the design of the stamping. Other details that determine cost are its shape, size, weight, the material of which it is made, the production process, and the other main characteristics. In addition, the quantities to be produced, specified tolerances and finishes also affect the cost. Finally, the available or necessary equipment for both building of the tools and for actual production are also part of the estimate.

Cost control is intimately related to cost estimating. After completion of each job, actual costs should be compared with estimated costs.

Every shop has a slightly different way to handle cost estimating. There is no standard procedure. This is one of the reasons why stamping customers receive such big differences in quotes.

The Basic Steps

There are certain basic steps in cost estimating which most metal stampers follow in a logical sequence in handling inquiries. The basic steps are these:

1) Determine whether or not to quote at all. This is often a managerial decision, not an entirely technical one
2) Check and double check the design tolerances, specifications, instructions: see Chapter 1
3) Determine production method (steps, equipment, inspection, etc.)
4) Establish tooling costs. This is usually noted separately from the stamping cost or piece price.
5) Establish both direct and indirect labor costs that can be allotted to the job in question
6) Establish stock cost
7) Determine cost of eventual services from suppliers
8) Add overhead

9) Add packaging, freight, and other supplementary expenses if applicable
10) Add profit.
Steps 4, 5, and 6 may be performed in any sequence; the other steps are taken in the sequence given.

Estimating Forms

It is general practice to use printed forms for estimates (1). In this way, there is no danger of overlooking some cost items. Since there is no standard form, every shop has its own form, developed and perfected from its own experience.

Design Requirements

To prepare a quote or cost estimate, it is necessary to be informed about the product. The characteristics expressed in the blueprint, specifications, and special instructions must be taken into account, including quantities per lot and total production.

Operation Line-Up

The actual quoting activity starts with conception and preparation of the *operation line-up* or manufacturing process. The operation line-up consists of all the technological steps needed to transform a piece of sheet metal into a stamping. The planning of the operation line-up consists in devising the simplest, most efficient way to produce the desired stamping. Every phase of production, from the receiving of raw material to shipping of the finished product must be considered. All the subsequent steps of the estimating process are influenced by the operation line-up.

Procedure. An operation line-up is prepared according to the following sequence:
1) Checking the stamping design
2) Determining the optimum production structure, i.e., kind, quantity, and sequence of single operations. The correct routing and sequence of operations is essential for troublefree and efficient production flow.
3) Performing mathematical computations for size, forces, pressures, etc.
4) Selecting equipment such as presses, tools, devices, gages
5) Finally, filling out the operation sheet with all the pertinent data. This may be a separate sheet or incorporated in the estimating form.
On the operation sheet the following data must be reported in addition to that indicated above:
1) Kind of stock needed and its identification by code number
2) Size of stock such as thickness, width, and progression
3) Shape of stock such as unit pieces, strips, coils, sheets
4) Quantity of stock needed per unit, per thousand, per lot
5) Production rates for every operation
6) Labor-skill specification—inspection method and means if nonstandard.
If more than one press stroke is needed for an operation, indicate it expressly. Otherwise it is assumed that only one press stroke is necessary. On the other hand, specify whether one or more operations are performed at any

given press-stroke such as whether multiplex and/or progressive and/or compound dies are being used. Specify whether one or more workpieces are produced at a given press stroke. If nothing is said about it, it is understood that one stamping is produced at every press stroke. Specify how many operators are needed for every operation. Otherwise it is assumed that only one operator is needed.

Tooling

Cost estimating of dies belongs decidedly to tool engineering. A few basic concepts follow: Cost of press-tools depends on the stamping design, tool design, tool construction, and shop facilities. The influence of stamping design depends on size, difficulties of production, surface finish, tolerances, and quantities. Influence of tool design depends on quantities, operation line-up, characteristics of press, and delivery dates. The influence of equipment depends on feeding and removal, whether manual, semiautomatic, or fully automatic. Add an amount for checking gages, if they are necessary. Also take into account tool maintenance costs.

Stock

The quantity of raw material needed for a given stamping depends first on the workpiece itself, on the production line-up, on the quantities to be produced, and on the original shape or quality of acquisition stock.

The material must be utilized at maximum efficiency as related to both surface and strength. If allowed, change the shape in order to be able to employ a lower overall quantity of stock. Scrapless design of stampings is possible only up to .060 in. stock thickness; otherwise the sides become too rough and too tapered.

The estimator must know commercial standard sizes and tolerances for the standard and special metals used for stampings — also the market prices paid for them by the shop. Stock prices go up with higher quality metal sheet, especially for formability. In case of progressive tooling, sometimes it is better to include an extra operation or station and use lower price stock; in the case of compound tooling, just the opposite is true.

If quantities can be justified, preference should be given to coils over strips and/or sheets. Prefinished materials save on finishing costs.

Material is figured at average costs. Use nominal, mean weights (see manufacturer's tables). Checking the actual weight of every batch of stock separately would only increase the control cost activity without giving substantial benefit from the greater accuracy. Use average cts/lb prices taken between extremes of low and high costs.

Labor

Labor cost is the sum of direct labor, indirect labor, die setting, tool maintenance, etc.

Direct labor is calculated by means of standard rates derived from similar work (Time and Motion Study helps in this respect). Indirect labor is figured as a percentage of direct labor. Indirect labor includes: supervision, inspection, material handling, plant maintenance, shipping and receiving, etc.

NOTE: If some operation, e.g., annealing between redrawings is foreseen only as a precaution, its cost should be indicated separately and the customer notified of the possibility of eliminating it.

Allied Operations

Stampings are sometimes submitted to some ulterior operation after they leave the last press. Such after-treatment operations are listed in Chapter 5.

Burden or Overhead

After reporting all the cost details on the standard quotation form, the overhead must be added.

There is no standard cost estimating procedure. Every shop follows its own pattern. The differences are attributable to the different ways of considering overhead. It is a simple matter to establish the cost of material; labor per unit cost is not difficult to estimate. But, on the question of overhead, differences of opinion range widely.

The many things that comprise overhead can be clearly enumerated: everything that does not bear direct relation to actual production, i.e., that which cannot be charged directly against a given product or job. But, the difficult task is to determine the cost of each overhead item, as well as to evaluate the whole complex of overhead.

In order to simplify the assignment of overhead charges, it is customary to use a percentage of either the whole basic cost or the direct labor cost, e.g., 150 to 200 percent.

For more accurate estimating, individual burden rates are established for each machine and production equipment type. The cost accounting department should figure these machine-hour rates. The real distribution of cost can be seen only by determining a separate overhead rate for each kind of production equipment. For this purpose so-called "cost centers" are established. Pieces of equipment roughly similar in performance, capacity or size, and financial value are grouped to form cost centers. For each cost center, its individual hourly charge is established based on past experience and kept up to date periodically. This rate takes care of depreciation, taxes, insurance, interests on invested capital, etc. Sometimes it also includes direct labor cost.

The cost of a stamping can be determined by taking the sum of all the items so far examined. To this, the profit must be added for both captive shops and job shops.

Profit

It is the Sales Department's responsibility to establish the selling price. Cost of sales, including salesman's commissions, cost of billing and auditing, etc. are included in the estimate as a relatively fixed percentage of the final cost.

There are some quoters who consider that the selling price is, in a way, independent from the estimated or checked cost of a product. According to this thinking, the selling price should be the highest that the market allows, i.e., the relationship between demand and offer at a given moment. There is no argument with this attitude as long as it is successful, i.e., as long as an estimator judges correctly the overall market situation. But even in such cases, a carefully prepared cost estimate should help greatly in deciding the right quoting price.

Whenever possible, it is good practice to let the salesman examine the estimate before a quote is sent to the customer.

Accuracy of Estimating

There are two schools of opinion on the accuracy of estimating. One group says: Every detail must be examined and calculated with the highest possible precision; inaccuracies will creep in anyway, but at least the start should be correct. The other group says: It is useless to do a lot of highly accurate computations, if eventually an uncertain quantity for burden must be added, defeating the accuracy of the whole procedure.

As always in such controversial situations, the best solution is a reasonable compromise. *Important factors* should be determined very accurately; the rest only approximately. Two dominating factors are: (1) stock in every case, and (2) tooling and labor in very short run jobs.

Calculations of *economical convenience* for given operational line-ups can be made only if two or more different line-ups are available. Whenever possible, make several operation line-ups for important, high-quantity stamping jobs, in order to choose the most convenient one.

Quoter's Tools

Since the quoter or estimator must complete many estimates daily, he should be supplied with proper tools. These tools are, first of all, accurate and detailed information about past stampings produced in his own shop—not estimates, but actual computations of stamping costs made after delivery. This information must come chiefly from company files, but may also come from the estimator's own experience. In case of new kinds of stampings for which there is no experience, it is also convenient to take advantage of data found in trade literature.

In order to speed up the quoting activity and to make it more exact, the data in the files should be collected systematically in tables, charts, nomograms, graphs, etc. for easy reference. These charts or data sheets should be made for:

1) Each basic tool type with toolmaker's hours needed for making them and the factors which critically affect basic toolmaker labor
2) Stampings: minimal hole sizes, locations of holes, maximum protrusion sizes, minimal bending radii, drawing reductions, etc.
3) Direct labor rates for each operation type and also in accordance with cost centers
4) Set-up charges according to operation, size, accessories, etc.
5) The estimator must have, in addition, a complete and detailed, up-to-date file showing:
   a. The facilities of the shop with detailed characteristics
   b. The operations that may be performed on each press and degree of accuracy
   c. Quantity and quality of skilled employees
   d. Every existing tool with every characteristic, especially those with universal character such as punching, notching, and embossing.

Shortcuts

In every company, there are some basic *ratios* which must be established and kept up to date:
1) Direct labor vs indirect labor. A good average is: 2 to 1
2) Labor cost vs total cost. Direct labor is usually 15 to 25 percent
3) Stock cost vs total cost. Average: 50 to 65 percent
4) Factory overhead vs total cost (15 to 20 percent)
5) Sales cost vs total cost (3 to 5 percent).

REFERENCES

1. Ivan R. Vernon, ed., *Realistic Cost Estimating for Manufacturing* (Dearborn, Mich.: Society of Manufacturing Engineers, 1968), pp. 109–13.

appendix C

NEW, SIMPLIFIED FORMULAS FOR DEVELOPED ROUND SHELL BLANKS

Practically all of the theoretical formulas for calculating the diameter of flat blanks or discs for conversion into drawn round shells include some square and square root calculations. These formulas have been simplified for the most common shell shapes to facilitate their use and are presented in Figs. C–1 through C–16.

Theoretical Formula

$$D = \sqrt{d^2 + 4\,d\,h}$$

Simplified Formula

$$D = 1.12\,(d + h)$$

Fig. C–1.

Theoretical Formula

$$D = \sqrt{d_2^2 + 4\,d_1\,h}$$

Simplified Formula

$$D = 0.7\,(d_1 + d_2 + h)$$

Fig. C–2.

Theoretical Formula

$$D = \sqrt{d_2^2 + 4\,(d_1 h_1 + d_2 h_2)}$$

Simplified Formula

$$D = 0.75\,(d_1 + d_2 + h_1 + h_2)$$

Fig. C–3.

Theoretical Formula

$$D = \sqrt{d_3^2 + 4\,(d_1 h_1 + d_2 h_2)}$$

Simplified Formula

$$D = 0.55\,(d_1 + d_2 + h_1 + h_2)$$

Fig. C–4.

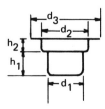

173

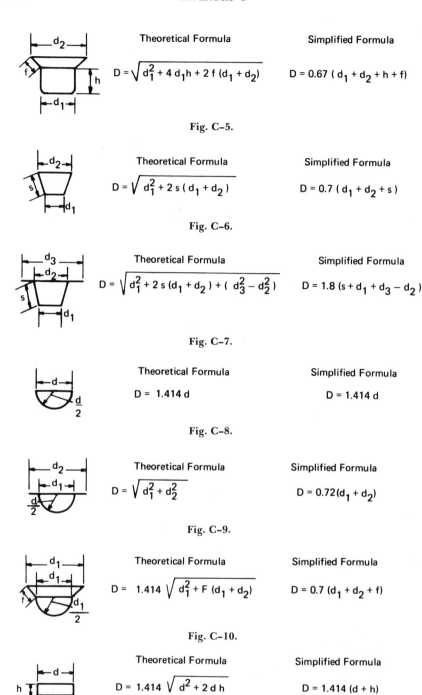

Theoretical Formula

$$D = \sqrt{d_1^2 + 4 d_1 h + 2 f (d_1 + d_2)}$$

Simplified Formula

$$D = 0.67 (d_1 + d_2 + h + f)$$

Fig. C–5.

Theoretical Formula

$$D = \sqrt{d_1^2 + 2 s (d_1 + d_2)}$$

Simplified Formula

$$D = 0.7 (d_1 + d_2 + s)$$

Fig. C–6.

Theoretical Formula

$$D = \sqrt{d_1^2 + 2 s (d_1 + d_2) + (d_3^2 - d_2^2)}$$

Simplified Formula

$$D = 1.8 (s + d_1 + d_3 - d_2)$$

Fig. C–7.

Theoretical Formula

$$D = 1.414 d$$

Simplified Formula

$$D = 1.414 d$$

Fig. C–8.

Theoretical Formula

$$D = \sqrt{d_1^2 + d_2^2}$$

Simplified Formula

$$D = 0.72 (d_1 + d_2)$$

Fig. C–9.

Theoretical Formula

$$D = 1.414 \sqrt{d_1^2 + F (d_1 + d_2)}$$

Simplified Formula

$$D = 0.7 (d_1 + d_2 + f)$$

Fig. C–10.

Theoretical Formula

$$D = 1.414 \sqrt{d^2 + 2 d h}$$

Simplified Formula

$$D = 1.414 (d + h)$$

Fig. C–11.

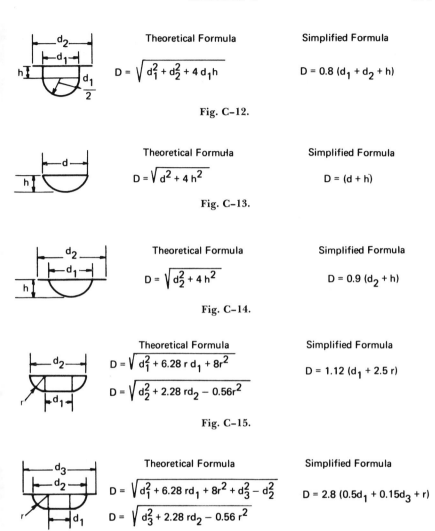

Theoretical Formula

$$D = \sqrt{d_1^2 + d_2^2 + 4 d_1 h}$$

Simplified Formula

$$D = 0.8 (d_1 + d_2 + h)$$

Fig. C–12.

Theoretical Formula

$$D = \sqrt{d^2 + 4 h^2}$$

Simplified Formula

$$D = (d + h)$$

Fig. C–13.

Theoretical Formula

$$D = \sqrt{d_2^2 + 4 h^2}$$

Simplified Formula

$$D = 0.9 (d_2 + h)$$

Fig. C–14.

Theoretical Formula

$$D = \sqrt{d_1^2 + 6.28 r d_1 + 8r^2}$$

$$D = \sqrt{d_2^2 + 2.28 rd_2 - 0.56r^2}$$

Simplified Formula

$$D = 1.12 (d_1 + 2.5 r)$$

Fig. C–15.

Theoretical Formula

$$D = \sqrt{d_1^2 + 6.28 rd_1 + 8r^2 + d_3^2 - d_2^2}$$

$$D = \sqrt{d_3^2 + 2.28 rd_2 - 0.56 r^2}$$

Simplified Formula

$$D = 2.8 (0.5d_1 + 0.15d_3 + r)$$

Fig. C–16.

The values given by the simplified formulas vary from those values obtained with the theoretical formulas by a slight variation of plus or minus a few percentage points. However, the traditional formulas do not take into consideration several factors which cannot be expressed numerically and which often cause substantial differences between theoretical data and actual data obtained in the press room.

Here is a list of such variable factors which are mostly uncontrollable:
1) Kind of stock and its physical properties, such as hardness, ductility, elongation, surface conditions, etc.
2) Shape of the blank, depth of draw vs size of bottom, ratio of shell diameter to corner radii

3) Surface conditions of the tool members, die clearance, corner radii, number of redrawings, etc.
4) Stock thickness
5) Blankholding method, blankholding pressure
6) Lubrication
7) Drawing speed.

index

A

Accuracy, cost estimating, 171
Adhesives, assembly by, 71
Alignment, 37
Alignment of stampings, 99–106
  axial, 104
  bushings, 108
  high accuracy, 101–104
  low accuracy, 99–100
  medium accuracy, 100–101
  spacer, 104–106
Alignment, tabs, 30–31
American National Standards Institute, 77
American Welding Society, 77
Anchorage, 40, 135–138
ANSI Standard (ANS Y 14.10–1959),
  115–116 (see also American National
  Standards Institute)
Arc-welded joints, 80–84
Assembled components, conversion from,
  148–149
Assembly (see Mechanical assembly;
  Welded assembly)
  stacked stampings, 66–72
Assembly methods, stacked stampings,
  66–72
  adhesives, 71
  brazing, 67
  drive fit, 66
  drive screws, 68
  groove pins, 66
  hot rivet, 66
  roll pins, 68
Axial alignment, 104

B

Bayonet-lock joint, 29
Bayonet locks, 96–98
Bends, compound, 56
Blanking die, round, 131
Blanks, nesting, 126–129
Bonded joints, stress relieving, 94–95
Brackets, tab design, 31
Brazing process, 67
Brazed joints, 73–77
Buffing, 114
Burden or overhead, 170
Burr height, 17
Burrs, 17–18
Bushings, alignment, 108

C

Cast workpieces, conversion from, 144–
  145
Chamfering, 21
Circular components, 45
Cleaning, 113
Combined shapes, 56
Combining machining and press
  operations, 149–151
Commercial quality, 134
Composite construction, 45
Composite design, metal stamping, 139–
  143
Compound bends, 56
Connectors, spring-slip, 33
Conversion to stamping technique,
  144–149

Conversion to stamping technique
   (*Continued*)
   from assembled components, 148–149
   from cast workpieces, 144–145
   from machined components, 146–147
Corrugations, 45
Cost centers, 170
Cost control, 167
Cost estimating, 167–172
   accuracy, 171
   cost centers, 170
   dies, cost of, 169
   form, 168
   labor
      direct, 169
      indirect, 169
   operations line-up, 168
   overhead, 170
   prefinished materials, 169
   procedure, cost estimating, 170
   profit, 170–171
   ratios, basic, 172
   sales department, 170–171
   stock, cost of, 169
   time and motion study, 169
Counterboring, 20–22
Countersinking, 20–22, 137
Crimped joints, 87–90
Crimped unions, 63
Crimping, 138
Curling, 53, 59–60, 129
Cyanidizing. 113

D

Design
   flat stampings, 8
      blanked, 14
      shaped, 13
      stamped links, 8–13
   formed stamping, 14–15
      bent parts, 14
      drawn shells and boxes, 14–15
      formed boxes, 14
      stacked stampings, 15
   tab (*see* Tab design)
Design, checklist for, 7–8
   blueprints, 7
   specifications, 7, 8
Design, minimum scrap, 45
   semiscrapless, 117
Die plate
   standard, 42
   closed, 44
Dies, cost of, 169
Dimensional tolerances, 111
   dies, 111
   press-brakes, 111

Drawing, severe, metals, 7
Drawn parts, 129–134
Drawn shells, 112, 138
Drive fit assembly, 66
Drive screws, hardened, 68
Ductility limit, 36
Ductility testing machine, 36

E

Embedding, inserts, 135–138
Embossing, 34–37
   boss diameter, 35
   bulge depth limits, 36–37
   cross-sectional shape, 35
   determining factors, 34
   forming process, 36
   location of boss, 36
   rounding radii, 35
   rubber forming dies, 36
   stock thinning, 36
Epoxy resin adhesives, 71
Estimating, cost, 167–172
   accuracy, 171
   cost centers, 170
   dies, cost of, 169
   form, 168
   labor
      direct, 169
      indirect, 169
   operations line-up, 168
   overhead, 170
   prefinished materials, 169
   procedure, cost estimating, 170
   profit, 170–171
   ratios, basic, 172
   sales department, 170–171
   stock, cost of, 169
   time and motion study, 169
Estimating form, 168
Euler's equation, 54
Extruded holes, 137
Extruded holes, bosses of, 104
Extrusions, partial, 37

F

Fastening, 38'
Ferrous metals, 5
Flanges, interrupted, 97
Flanging, 54–56, 138
Flat blanks, 117–124
Flat stamping design, 8
   blanked, 14
   shaped, 13
   stamped links, 8–13
Flat stampings, 109–111
Folding, assembly by, 90–93

Formed stamping design, 14–15
  bent parts, 14
  drawn shells and boxes, 14–15
  formed boxes, 14
  stacked stampings, 15
Formed stampings, 111
Forming, 41
Formulas
  full shaft, 161–165
  hollow shaft, 161–165
  theoretical and simplified, 173–176

G

Groove pins, 66

H

Heat treatment, 112–113
Hemming, 53, 60–61
Hole, land of, 19
Holes, 117–124
  ANSI Standard (ANS Y 14.10–1959), 115–116
  countersunk, 137
Holes, extruded, 22–26
  alignment, 25
  assembly, 22–25
  bearings, 25
  calculations, 26–28
  miscellaneous, 26
  other than round bosses, 26
  protection, 25–26
  reinforcing, 25
  theoretical height, 27
Holes, in stampings, 18–19
  nonround, 18
  round, 18
Hot rivet, 26

I

Inserts, anchorage, 40
Inserts, metal, 135–139
Internal stresses, avoidance of, 135

J

Joggling, 56
Joints
  arc-welded, 80–84
  brazed, 73–77
  projection, welded, 77–80

K

Knurling, 138

L

Labor
  direct, 169
  indirect, 169
Laminations, 17
Land, 19, 20
Loads
  bending, 53
  buckling, 53
Locking methods, 153–155
  permanent, 155
  reuseable, 153–155
Lock seam, 85

M

Machined components, conversion from, 146–147
Machining, 113
Material
  quality, 114–115
  strength of, 53
  thickness, 115
Materials for stamping, 4–7
  ferrous metals, 5
  metals for drawing and severe drawing, 7
  nonferrous metals, 6
  nonmetallic materials, 6
  prefinished metal sheets, 6
Mechanical assembly, 84–98
  bayonet locks, 96–98
  crimped joints, 87–90
  folding, assembly by, 90–93
  seams, 84–87
    lock seam, 85
    simple, 85
Metal stampings, 3
Milling stampings, 151
Minimum scrap, 45

N

Nesting, blanks, 126–129
Nitriding, 113
Nonferrous metals, 6
Nonmetallic materials, 6

O

Operations line-up, 168
Overhead, burden, 170

P

Panels, corrugated, 58–59
Paper fasteners, 90

Partial extrusions, 37
Partial punching, 37
Penetration, punch, 41
Permanent unions, 38
Pins, groove, 66
Pivoting, 40
Prefinished materials, 169
Prefinished metal sheets, 6
Press operations, 149–151
Pressworking, 167
Procedure, cost estimating, 170
Profit, 170–171
Projection welded joints, 77–80
Projection welding, 63
Protrusions, 37–44, 104, 137
    alignment, 37
    anchorage, 40
    fastening, 38
    forming, 41
    partial extrusions, 37
    partial punching, 37
    pivoting, 40
    retained slug forming, 37
    rivet lug forming, 37
    semi-perf, 37
    separating, 39
Protuberance, 129
Punch, stepped, 43
Punch-penetration, 41 (table), 42
Punching die, 41
Punching, partial, 37

R

Ratios, basic cost estimating, 172
Reinforcing processes, 45, 53–65
    bending, 53
    combined shapes, 56
    compound bends, 56
    corrugated panels, 58–59
    curling, 53, 59–60
    flanging, 54–56
    hemming, 53, 60–61
    joggling, 56
    rib-forming, 53
    ribs, 57, 64
    ribs, function of, 62–65
    rigidized sheets, 62
    seaming, 53, 61
Retained slug forming, 37
Ribs, 57, 64
Ribs, function of, 62–65
Rigidity increase (table), 62
Rigidized sheets, 62
Rivet, hot, 66
Rivet lug forming, 37
Roll pins, 68

S

Sales department, 170–171
Scrapless design, 46
Seaming, 53, 61
Seams, basic design of, 84–87
    lock seam, 85
    simple, 85
Semi-perf, 37
Severe drawing, metals, 7
Shafts, 161–165
    formulas, 161–165
    full, 161–165
    hollow, 161–165
Shelving, boltless, 32–33
Shot peening, 114
Slug, severance, 42
Spacers, 39
Stacked stampings, 66–72
Stacking, 17, 45
Stamping, materials for, 4–7
    ferrous metals, 5
    metals for drawing and severe
        drawing, 7
    nonferrous metals, 6
    nonmetallic materials, 6
    prefinished metal sheets, 6
Stamping technique, conversion to,
    144–149
Stampings
    composite design, 139–143
    flanged (table), 56
    formed, 124–126
    milling of, 151
    scrapless design, 46, 47, 51
Stampings, alignment of, 99–106
    axial, 104
    bushings, 108
    high accuracy, 101–104
    low accuracy, 99–100
    medium accuracy, 100–101
    spacer, 104–106
Stampings, stacked, 65–72
    assembly methods, 66–72
        adhesives, 71
        brazing, 67
        drive fit, 66
        drive screws, 68
        groove pins, 66
        hot rivet, 66
        roll pins, 68
Standardization, stamping design, 114
    holes, 115–116
    material, quality, 114–115
        thickness, 115
    strip width, 115
Steel, commercial quality, 134
Stock, cost of, 169

Stock thickness, 112
Stop plate, 153, 154, 155
Stress relief, 106–109
Strip width, 115
Surface treatment, 113–114

Tabs, design, 28–34
  alignment, 30–31
  boltless shelving, 32–33
  brackets, 31
  fastening, 28
  internal, 28
  miscellaneous, 33
  shear-formed (lanced), 28, 137
Temporary assemblies, 63
Time and motion study, 169
Tolerances, metal stamping, 109–114
  dimensional, average
    dies, 111
    press-brakes, 111

Tolerances, metal stamping
  (*Continued*)
  drawn shells, 112
  flat stampings, 109–111
  formed stampings, 111
  stock thickness, 112
Tote boxes, 33
Tube, short lengths, 138
Tumbling, 113–114
Twisting, 129

Vapor blasting, 113

W

Welded assembly, 73–84
  arc-welded joints, 80–84
  brazed joints, 73–77
  projection welded joints, 77–80
Welding, projection, 63

Other Books from SME . . .

Manufacturing Data Series

Adhesives in Modern Manufacturing
Cold Bending and Forming Tube and Other Sections
Cutting and Grinding Fluids: Selection and Application
Cutting Tool Material Selection
Design of Cutting Tools: Use of Metal Cutting Theory
Functional Gaging of Positionally Toleranced Parts
Functional Inspection Techniques
Fundamentals of Position Tolerance
Gundrilling, Trepanning, and Deep
Hole Machining (Revised Edition)
High-Velocity Forming of Metals (Revised Edition)
Jigs and Fixtures for Limited Production
Machining the Space-Age Metals
Non-Traditional Machining Processes
Pneumatic Controls for Industrial Application
Premachining Planning and Tool Presetting
Producibility/Machinability of Space-Age
and Conventional Materials
Realistic Cost Estimating for Manufacturing
Tool Engineering: Organization and Operation

Numerical Control Series

Introduction to Numerical Control in Manufacturing
N/C Machinability Data Systems

Manufacturing Management Series

Introduction to Manufacturing Management
Organization for Manufacturing
Modern Aspects of Manufacturing Management: Selected Readings

For further information, write to: Publication Sales Department
Society of Manufacturing Engineers
20501 Ford Road
Dearborn, Michigan 48128